Living the Egyptian Dream

A Middle-Aged Woman's Gap Year

by
Margaret Rowswell

Eloquent Books
New York, New York

Eloquent Books
An imprint of AEG Publishing Group
845 Third Avenue, 6th Floor – 6016
New York, NY 10022
www.eloquentbooks.com

ISBN: 978-1-60693-600-9   1-60693-600-X

Printed in the United States of America

Cover Design: Peggy Ann Rupp, *www.netdbs.com*

Book Design: D. Johnson, Dedicated Business Solutions, Inc.

Dedication

For Louisa and Claudine, my darling daughters, who never did really understand my need, but who still unfailingly supported it; and for all my long-suffering friends whose love and kindness meant so much. This is also for Galal, who kept me laughing no matter what, and whose continuing friendship I value highly.

Living the Egyptian Dream

A Middle-Aged Woman's Gap Year

Foreword

After a period of my life when many things had gone awry, I decided that the best way forward would be to spend a long period of time at my flat in Luxor where I could complete my convalescence after surgery and generally regroup and rethink my life.

I had always had a pull to Egypt, as indeed do many people. The history of the country had always been a source of fascination to me and when I had visited for the first time in 1993, I was just blown away by what I saw. Consequently, I kept going back for more! After successive visits, I found the Egyptian people totally endearing and their approach to life so different from ours in the West. Of necessity the heat makes the pace of life slower, but their philosophy is that nothing is ever a problem and everything is totally possible, which I found refreshing after the negativity of Western thinking.

It had been a natural progression from going on copious holidays to Luxor to buying a flat there for holiday use, and so at this particular turning point in my life, it was the obvious place to go to. I had undergone fairly major surgery, simultaneous to handing in my notice at work. This had not been a conscious decision to do the two things at the same time, but was a strange quirk of fate that it happened that way! I therefore found myself with only temporary work through the summer and it seemed like a God-given opportunity to do something completely different, to take a gap year in effect, take a breathing space, look at life, and decide on the way ahead.

Of course that decision involved parting from the family I adored—my two daughters, their husbands, and three gorgeous grandchildren, together with all my friends—but this wasn't going to be forever. There were telephones, mobiles, emails, computer phones, and Web-cams and there was really no need to lose touch with anyone. It was an opportunity

1

I couldn't let pass. It felt like a "now or never" opportunity. Having been brought up as an only child, who always did the right thing and always did as she was told, was seldom seriously naughty and always toed the line, a little bit of the rebel in me came wandering to the surface! If I didn't take the opportunity when I was without a permanent job and in need of a little convalescence, then I was going to get stuck back into the rat race of a nine to five existence—getting up, going to work, coming home and going to bed! No, it *had* to be now!

My intention in writing a diary whilst I was there was initially for myself. I wanted to remember it as it was, warts and all. I didn't want to look back at it through rose-coloured spectacles and think of it as a time of enchantment in which nothing went wrong. I needed to remember the good and the bad. Having reached this decision, it then seemed a nice thing to write it also for my two daughters, so that they could see what their mother was up to. It was never my intention to write it for anyone else.

However, having started the diary, many friends asked if they could read it, and I found myself emailing installments left, right, and centre! The feedback I got was extremely positive. In fact, they kept asking for more!

It became quite therapeutic, especially on the days where things had been trying: the more irritating the incident, the faster the fingers flew over the keyboard! The fact that other people might be enjoying it was just a bonus.

Should others, by reading my experiences, come to Luxor and enjoy the charms and delight that make Egypt what it is, then my writing will have been for very good purpose.

October

Euphoria, disbelief, fear. The full range of emotions ran through my first day. I could hardly believe that I had actually achieved it. My UK flat was let with delightful tenants, and I was safely installed in my flat in Luxor.

It felt like a month since I'd had a really good night's sleep. Initially, worry and disappointment had kept me up. The task of finding a suitable tenant for my flat seemed insurmountable. And after I'd found those elusive tenants, the frenzy of packing up my whole life in a fortnight robbed me of sleep.

My friends' support was indescribable and they were all quite amazing. Once my roof space was full, huge bags of linen and various belongings made their way to a friend; and another friend, returning from her holiday in Canada, found she had an unexpected houseguest for three nights before my flight to Egypt. She kept me calm and grounded during that time of intense excitement and more than a smidgen of apprehension.

The move out of my flat had proved more expensive than originally budgeted, with electrical tests and a certificate required; and worst of all, any soft furnishings that did not carry a fire-retardant label had to leave the building. This necessitated the hasty purchase of a new three-piece suite and the rapid departure of the old one. My flexible friend was almost bent double as my continuing expenditure grew!

However, the day finally dawned for my departure to Luxor. My friend, J, took me to the airport, gallantly accompanying me to check in—in case there were any difficulties with my two enormous suitcases, which had been pre-booked and paid for. How fortunate that she was there. My first case weighed the maximum allowed for one item; the second—disaster!—I had to loose three kg. Soon the padlock was undone and the zips unzipped, as I maniacally searched through my oh-so-carefully-packed case to find something suitably heavy to offload. A handbag, a jacket, and jumpers packed

3

for the chilly desert nights of January were flung out by my demented person, and—bingo!—yes, all was well. My long-suffering friend bade me a fond farewell and left Gatwick with a carrier bag full of my things, ready to be passed on to my first visitor in a couple of months, who would bring it with her as excess baggage.

I endured the usual time-passing, and then we were boarding. I sat beside a young couple on their first visit to Egypt. They were good company, and we exchanged phone numbers for a possible meet up during their stay. The flight was peppered with unusual occurrences: a lightening storm, which was quite beautiful to watch, and then a storm of my own when my vegetarian meal had not been booked and there wasn't a spare one to give me. The meal was chicken, the one meat that I never eat. My delightful companions gave me their rolls and cheese in exchange for my milk and sugar, and together we attempted the lemon pudding with courage and a fixed smile on our faces! Finally, coming in to land, the landing cards were distributed, but wait! These all had to be handed back in, as they were the wrong ones and we would have to fill them in again at the airport!

My laptop safely in my backpack, I felt as if I would fall flat on my back as the bus jostled us across the tarmac. Would my two cases be there? Or would the hastily re-jigged second case have burst its zips, causing my knickers to come sailing round the carousel ahead of it? All was well: both were there, although a luggage strap had gone AWOL, and a wonderful Good Samaritan heaved both of them off the carousel for me and loaded up my trolley. His reward will surely be in heaven, as my grandmother was wont to say.

Wheeling all my worldly goods to the door, I could see Mr. F. waiting for me outside, and off we set in his awaiting taxi. The young lad who always carries the luggage was waiting. He always looks as though a puff of wind would blow him over, but his strength is positively Samsonite! Up four flights of stairs he went with my Big Bertha suitcase perched on one shoulder, his head precariously tilted to one side. I swear he was four inches smaller after the second case!

Another night's sleep eluded me, as exhaustion and an overactive mind fought each other. Then it was morning, the FIRST morning of my temporary new life. Where on earth would I start? I had the bathroom and kitchen to clean to European standards, everything to unpack, and food shopping to do.

I started with the bathroom and kitchen, followed by a coffee. There was so much unpacking and sorting out to do that it took most of the day in easy stages. I made a phone call to my favourite taxi driver, and we were off to Omar's, the supermarket. Fruit and vegetables came next, and then a hunt for more coat hangers. Then back to the flat, where the noble taxi driver helped me carry my many bags up the four flights so that it was done in one go.

Shopping put away, I had a new list written of things to shop for with my German friend in Luxor. As she was a shopper as dedicated as myself, we had much to accomplish. A quick phone call and a few text messages established that she was up for the challenge!

Next came a shower, a Pimm's, and a short walk down to the Mercure Hotel to treat myself to dinner out. Feeling tired again, I battled with the TV and the DVD player and lost on both counts. I made a phone call to Mr. F.—a friend of a friend to whom I had been introduced on a previous visit some months earlier—who made arrangements for his son to come and help me the next day to start the process of getting me online.

More tired than should be possible, my first day came abruptly to an end, as the need for sleep was paramount and was enabling those negative feelings of self-doubt to creep in. Surely one must be able to sleep eventually, and then the new challenges ahead should resume their positivity.

I awoke after ten hours of solid sleep, feeling like a completely different person. Two glasses of water and a glass of fruit juice re-hydrated the prune I felt I had become. I had the threat of a migraine, which was not surprising; the right side of my head was throbbing, and my neck was in spasm, so I took some tablets with my water and rubbed some Bio-freeze on my neck. By the time I decided on the caffeine fix, the pain was gone, and an overwhelming sense of happiness settled in its place. I felt surprisingly tearful. I remembered my mother telling me that she had cried over breakfast on the first morning of her honeymoon because she just felt so happy, and I could identify with the emotion. The many pho-tographs of my beloved children and grandchildren that are dotted round the flat gave rise to more tears—good heavens, whatever was the matter with me?

In an effort to put such emotional turmoil behind me, I prepared to clean. The disadvantage of living on the edge of a desert is the dust. Sand, sand, and yet more sand, all of which seemed to mix with the dust of the town to find its way into every crevice. The fight to keep things sparkly clean—as we expect in the West—is a never ending one. The flat is always cleaned before my arrival, but it is still always in need of a little European laundering. Three hours later, it was beginning to feel and look much better. The purchase of a new vacuum cleaner helped no end, and by now the bath-room was positively gleaming.

My brand new dishwasher was filled, the soap dispensed, and the instructions read. I pressed *start* . . . but there was no water! I turned taps, straightened hoses, re-read the in-structions, and pressed start again. Still no water. Plumbing, I have found, is an Egyptian conundrum. Every time I come, there is always some sort of plumbing problem. It is all read-ily solved, but it continues to happen. I added it to my list to ask Mr. F., along with the leaking toilet, the clogged tap in the bidet, the TV satellite card, and the non-working DVD player. He had already sent a man to fix the air-conditioning in the lounge, which he did in the blink of an eye, re-wiring it with the electricity turned on and charging me ten Egyptian pounds (10LE), equal to about £1! Mr. F.'s son had checked my computer in preparation for getting online, and whilst he was there, he fixed the tap in the bidet. The taps all have little filters on them which seem to get clogged up. A pair of pliers, a needle, and it was fixed!

With dinner to prepare, I decided on cauliflower cheese, only to realise I had nothing in the cupboard with which to thicken a sauce; tuna pasta bake it was, then! The next battle was with the cooker. Calor gas being a medium I am unfamiliar with, I tentatively reached for the lighter. Nothing. Undaunted, I turned the tap on the huge bottle of gas and tried again. Nothing. I tried a different burner. Nothing. A third burner—yes! So, finding two burners that worked, I cooked my first dinner with a successful outcome. I retried the initial two burners on the cooker, and for some extraordinary reason, they were now working perfectly. *Don't question*, I told myself, *just accept. This is Egypt.*

I made a trip to Mr. F.'s office, where he works every night until 10:00 p.m. His secretary, a young Egyptian girl, brought me lemonade, and we sat and talked. He gave me a book called *How to Learn English without a Teacher*. Mr. F. had learned his English with this book. He told me to learn five Arabic words every day and that he would help me with the pronunciation; then, by the end of seven months, I would have a good Arabic vocabulary. It was so kind of him, and learning Arabic was something I would love to be able to do, so I would try. He took my list of things to be fixed, and we arranged to meet on Saturday to get the phone line ordered and set up the box address at the post office. He walked me home, and we hit my next problem. The key would not open the front door. Eventually we got in and tested the lock again. It worked perfectly every time, but on the last try the problem repeated and the lock flipped back out, effectively re-locking the door. I was told I was being too gentle with it, but that someone would be dispatched to check it for me in a day or two. Anxiety every time I went out loomed ahead—what if I couldn't get back in? But for now, to bed.

Sleep, the great healer. After another nine hours of solid slumber, I awoke ready for the next set of challenges that the day would surely bring.

I started by cleaning the kitchen balcony. It was my favourite place to sit, with its magical view across the Nile to the mountains beyond and the hidden secrets of the West Bank. All was going well until I dropped the Hoover on my foot and a blue lump the size of a golf ball materialised almost instantly. I had a cupboard full of medical necessities; surely there was something there to help. Shades of my daughter's orthopaedic training and my own administrative orthopaedic sojourn crossed my mind: RICE—rest, ice, compression, elevation. Not all of them were appropriate in this case, but rest, arnica, and elevation did the trick. An hour later, I was amazed to see that my foot had almost returned to its normal shape, with only the hint of a bruise. There was a lesson to be learned here. I must be more careful; a fall or more serious injury would not be so easily solved.

Onwards with the ironing. Why are chores so much more pleasurable here? I hate ironing, but this morning it was positively fun! The answer has to be time. The usual pace of day-to-day life just isn't the same here. I am not forever chasing my tail; my time is my own; I have no commitments and no schedule to keep. I feel like a little girl playing house, where everything is fun and the nesting instinct is strong to make everything perfect.

I had a phone call from Mr. F. to say that his son would arrive with various workmen at 5:30 p.m. to look at the dishwasher, DVD and TV, the front door lock, and the air-conditioning unit, which had again stopped, despite its new wiring.

With that in mind, I decided on the task of the day: find the post office, buy a stamp, and post a letter. I set out with sense of purpose. For some reason I have yet to learn, nearly every street in Luxor is being dug up at the moment. It was like walking down the beach, wading through sand and dodging the traffic. The trick was to walk on regardless, as the Egyptians do, the premise being that cars have steering and brakes and will avoid you. It seems to work, but one has to close the mind to the instilled Green Cross Code of one's youth. I found the post office, bought my stamp, and posted my letter, wondering how long it would take to reach its UK destination.

Inspired by my achievement, I decided to try the government shop for a few household items. I was greeted warmly and miraculously left alone when I said I just wanted to look. I had to step over a man sitting on some marble steps having his *siesta*. In the next room, I found another, similarly comatosed on his counter. Unsuccessful in my search, I decided to wait until I was with my German friend on our shopping expedition. For now, I continued onwards to the small supermarket near the flat. It was suddenly windy, and I found half the sand of the street deposited in my eye under a contact lens. In my discomfort, and in an effort to avoid an overly friendly local, I found I had walked past the shop. A quick turn around, and I entered the shop, right eye streaming and thus attracting much more attention than I wished for. Despite being told that I would find "everything what you want in here," I didn't find very much. I did find some sugar, milk, and the elusive corn flour, which was a welcome surprise—cauliflower cheese would yet be mine! By now I was hot, very, very hot, and struggling to carry my parcels, which were upsetting my tennis elbow. With a passing thought for my G.P. that yes, I know rest is the answer, I switched hands and walked down the street chanting in my head that I would lose weight and I would get fit, like some sort of mantra. Up the four flights of stairs and a quick prayer to the "Angel of Locks and Keys" that my key would let me in. I turned the key with the determination and lack of delicacy that Mr. F. had insisted upon, and the door opened. Thank you.

A glance in the mirror showed me a scarlet-faced person. I checked the thermometer on the balcony: one-hundred-and-two degrees. Yes, I thought it was feeling warm today!

I received a phone call from Mr. F., confirming that his son would come at 5:30 p.m. with someone to fix the dishwasher. He arrived at 5:45 p.m., which was really quite punctual for Egyptian time, with no less than three men with him! One set to work on the computer and DVD, one on the front door, and one on the dishwasher and air-conditioner. This last one seemed a strange combination of talents, but no matter. The DVD was soon sorted, the problem only due to my own incapability with technological wiring, as I had suspected it would be; soon the various plugs were inserted in the correct places, and it was working. He then made ready for my Internet connection and gave me a nice icon on the desktop to make the connection. The opening menu asked for a username and password, but I was told this was not necessary, and I only had to click on connect. How I hoped he was right! I had not been at all happy with him looking into all my settings, so carefully configured in the UK, especially as he took off my desktop picture and then couldn't find it to put it back up. My confidence in this "specialist" was diminishing. However, I was assured that all was ready. So I had just the phone line to sort out on Saturday, and then I should be ready to connect.

The front door lock, of course, would not do its special trick of flicking back, but with great diligence the lock was removed and oiled and put through its paces. I could only keep my fingers crossed.

The dishwasher proved more of a problem, and the English spoken was insufficient to explain to me exactly what was wrong. This brand new piece of equipment obviously had a gremlin, but in true Egyptian fashion, everything was taken apart and stripped down, and in about forty minutes it was working perfectly. This versatile chap then turned his attentions to the air-conditioning unit, fixing it in an instant. It had been blowing the fuse, and I was shown which one to turn back on. I tried to ask why it was doing this so often, as clearly there was a problem here. The lack of English made the going tough, but my understanding was that the trip was too sensitive and it needed something bigger—a bigger fuse? I asked if it was dangerous, and they all assured me that it was not. Nonetheless, if it were to happen again, I was to contact Mr. F.'s son, and he would contact them and they would come and fix it. Mmmm??!!!

It was at this point that I found the satellite receiver was hot, despite the fact that it was no longer plugged in. Mr. F.'s son looked and felt it and shrugged.

"No problem."

"No problem? It was hot; might it catch fire?"

"No, no."

Really? There was much shaking of hands, £1 for the lock man, £6 between them for the computer man and the dishwasher man. And then they were gone.

I settled down to watch a DVD: *Jonathan Creek,* entertaining and relaxing with an accompanying brandy. However, sleep was not forthcoming that night, with thoughts of the hot satellite receiver and warnings from Mr. F. never to let anyone into my flat alone if they were not friends. His explanation that if I were killed, he would get the blame—as no one else knew me and he held my key—did nothing to calm my ever-churning mind that night!

I decided to throw in the towel on sleeping at 6:45 a.m. After a drink of juice, I decided to clean the balcony before it got too hot. It was a good decision in the relative cool of the early morning, and the task was done in an hour. I then had my breakfast and decided I had earned a swim. It was a delightful way to spend the morning. After wandering back for lunch, I arranged with my taxi driver to take me to the shop that some English friends have nicknamed Plastic Alley. I was hoping to meet my German friend for such a trip, but she rang in the morning to say that she had been without water all morning and must catch up on her chores now that it was back on. Undaunted, but disappointed not to see her, I decided I must go it alone.

The shop is a marvel. It is down a dirt side street and has merchandise spilling outside. Inside, it has three floors and resembles something of a charity shop in the UK. There is no real semblance of order; things are all over the place, and you must search with great determination for anything you need. It is quite an Aladdin's cave and holds no end of delights if one has the patience to search. I found a canister that I needed to keep my coffee in, but was told that I could only buy it in a set of three. More searching uncovered an alternative and another one for keeping pasta. Up a floor I found a plastic table, ideal for the kitchen balcony. Down two floors I bought some more coat hangers and a wooden stool for my dressing table. The total cost of my purchases £10. The driver met me outside and put everything in the taxi. His son had arrived; he was a boy of about twelve, who jumped in the front seat next to his father. We set off for home, stopping briefly on the way for the boy to hop out and buy me a bottle of water.

The inevitable cleaning followed. Everything you buy here is covered in the ever-present dust and needs to be washed and cleaned before use. This includes packets and tins purchased in the supermarkets. I was alarmed to hear from my German friend that one of the hotels had stopped buying their provisions from the supermarket I used, as they had been turning the electricity off at night! She warned me against buying any frozen food from there.

I put my newly purchased and cleaned small table on the kitchen balcony. Looking over, I saw four men from the adjacent museum lined up on their prayer mat, facing east and praying. There is often activity here, as they had recently opened a coffee shop in the museum, and this outside courtyard appeared to be part of the kitchen facility! The kitchen staff started quite early in the morning, sweeping and then preparing, and they are working through the day. Then at night they all sit round a table and eat together before closing and going home. A small fly on the wall insight into Egyptian working routines.

At 5:00 p.m. it was getting darker, and I put on the lights. The electricity here is a law unto itself. When I first took possession of the flat, I was forever changing light bulbs until I realised that the lights go up and down according to the power surges. Sometimes you have all the light bulbs working, sometimes half. Now I just accept it, although it always raises a smile. I went out on the large balcony to watch the sunset, but the day had been cloudy and there was nothing much to see. The late afternoon was pleasantly warm, lacking the enormous heat of the previous day. Mr. F. had told me that it gets cold on November 20. He was very precise and very certain about it. It would be interesting to see.

There are busy days, and then there are days like this one. I woke at 6:30 a.m. and decided to get up; I had a lot of things to do. At 9:00 a.m. there was a power cut. This, of course, affected the water, too. Undaunted, I went to the cash machine at the bank and took out my money for the long-awaited phone line. I looked at my remaining balance on the slip: £0—oops! Without getting online, it was impossible to move funds around, and this was a scenario I had hoped to avoid. I bought some water and took it back to the flat, and whilst there, the power came back on. I removed the towels I had hastily packed the freezer with to conserve the frozen food and set off to meet Mr. F.'s son outside the church.

I had an interesting five-minute wait for him, watching the comings and goings of the Coptic Church; the priest arrived, and everyone who could, grasped his hand and kissed it—I wondered how our local vicar in Sussex would take to this!

Mr. F.'s son arrived, and we set off for the telephone office. Through the usual sand and dust, I arrived with my feet caked. We met a cousin, a man, Mr. F. told me, who had had a heart attack earlier in the week, but was coming in to work especially to help me! I suspect he had had an angina attack, but who am I to say? Either way, I was eternally grateful to him. In Egypt nobody queues; you just walk up to the relevant counter and push in front of everyone else! I watched during the hour it took to sort everything out, and this indeed appeared to be the general way of things. The office was heaving with people, and a lot of bored children were accompanying the adults. All, I noticed with passing amusement, had feet similarly caked in wet sand to myself! My passport was shown, and we went outside to another office where I paid the fee and was given a choice of telephone numbers. I chose one that I hoped I could remember and was told that the line would be put in the next day, Sunday, in the evening.

On then to the post office to set up a box number. This was another hour spent shifting from counter to counter and various offices all over the building. I presented my passport again, and they made a copy, together with a copy of my visa, which always causes confusion as I have so many. I had the current one marked with a sticker, but still always had to indicate the correct one. Again, this extraordinary method of non-queuing! It seems quite acceptable, and even in the midst of a transaction, the counter clerk stops and deals with the person who has pushed in. No one gets aggravated by this. I suspect there is some sort of hierarchy, but it isn't obviously apparent. A little over an hour later, I had a post box number, and Mr. F.'s son said he would give me the key the next day. The place where the boxes are located is right at the back of the post office, down a grubby alley, which is also being dug up and requires some kind of mountaineering experience. Perhaps a weekly check on the post will be sufficient!

I went on to meet my German friend for lunch, and we went home via the supermarket. The queuing here—or lack of queuing!—is similar. You put your basket down, and whilst it is being checked out, if someone else comes along with a couple of items, they push their money towards the till and your transaction stops! It has crossed my mind that my shopping bill may be higher than necessary if other people's shopping is being added to my total! I had a cup of coffee at my friend's house and then took a taxi home.

Feeling more than a little tired, I decided to make some soup and watch the end of a DVD I had started the day before. No sooner had I started the soup than the electricity went off again. It was dark—very, very dark! Not yet as familiar with my surroundings as I would be in my UK flat, I groped around with the help of my mobile phone for light! I found a candle and some matches and wondered what I would do whilst waiting. It was only 7:00 p.m., a little early to sleep. The computer—ah yes, fully charged, it would now work from its batteries. I could write, I could play solitaire. After twenty minutes, deep joy! Everything returned as the power resumed. The welcome drone of the air-conditioning was best of all, as I had been trying to kid myself that it wasn't getting hot—but it really had taken only a few minutes for the cold air to disappear.

Thoughts of solitaire now behind me, I turned my attentions back to the soup, the DVD, and an early night.

On Sunday, I decided on a leisurely start. I sat on the kitchen balcony with some fruit juice, then made coffee and moved to the large balcony on the other side with my *Daily Mail* newspaper, which I had bought at enormous expense the day before. At £3, I decided I would read every word written, only to discover there were four pages missing from the centre! Not normally known for my gullibility, I had been severely conned on this occasion!

It was cool on the balcony with a light breeze; the sky was a brilliant, cloudless blue, and the mountains were clear across the Nile. The men building on the other side of the road were loudly mixing concrete, but even amidst the din, an overwhelming sense of calm and peace settled on me. This surely was what these seven months were all about. I didn't need to *do* anything, I just had to *be*. The words spoken at the end of the church service I would normally be attending at this time on a Sunday morning came into my head: "May the Peace of God, which passes all understanding . . ." This certainly was some sort of God-given peace that I truly didn't understand, but did experience at that moment.

I watched the road sweeper doing his best with the dust and sand at the entrance to the road. What a thankless and never-ending task! I looked at the huge pile of sand awaiting the builders at the side of the road. With a little more breeze, it would start covering his newly swept patch. The bin man came next. In place of the big lorries we have in Europe was a man pushing a small metal frame with two dustbins on it. One bag almost fills one bin, so he hangs the others over the frame and walks on, looking for more. The street is actually kept remarkably well this way. Any rubbish you have, you leave bagged up at the entrance to the building, and this little man spends his day wandering round, collecting it all up. A truck pulled up and several soldiers jumped out, others ambling up to the truck. Ah, the changing of the guard. I glanced at the time—7:30 a.m.—yes, this was obviously the day shift.

I decided on a little more retail therapy. I walked down the Corniche to Gaddis, where I knew I could buy a good quality tablecloth. It was easier walking down by the Nile and certainly cleaner underfoot. Walking by the Nile used to be impossible, as one was always followed and hassled by the felucca drivers, but a law had been passed forbidding them to tout this way for business. Of course that hadn't stopped it, but they only called out to you now and didn't fall into step with you, making it a pleasant walk. I bought my tablecloth and stopped for a drink at one of the hotels.

Wandering back, I spotted some small mugs at one of the bazaars and went in. The shopkeeper met me with enthusiasm, speaking excellent English with a slight Yorkshire twang! We discussed the price of the mugs, and he told me about their excellent quality. He decided I should have a drink whilst we talked about it. He brought in two plastic chairs and a tin of Coke, which, with great chivalry, he opened and wiped on his shirt for me! As I was drinking, he produced a pad and pen and asked me to write down a message for him so that he could send a text. After the second, quite long message, I told him I should be charging him because I was working! He enjoyed the joke, and we settled on a good price for the mugs.

I went home for lunch, happy with the outcome of my morning, and wondering whether I would indeed have my phone line put in later today. The afternoon quickly passed, and I spent the evening taking up a hem (I can't sew for toffee, goodness I was changing already!) and listening to Arabic television; could it be that I could pick some of it up subliminally? I wondered. Needless to say, there was no sign of the telephone line. I was beginning to panic. I had to be able to access my finances online. I was currently living on the cash in my purse, which wasn't going to last very much longer.

I went to bed anxious and inevitably woke up with a headache. As it was Monday, I decided that chores were the order of the day, but first sat with my fruit juice on the kitchen balcony. I watched the man from the museum kitchen doing the washing up with a hose! I was fascinated. First he cleared the table from their previous night's dinner. He started folding the tablecloth and then rolled it up. He put it on a wall in the shade and then sat on it! He had seven large containers that sat on frames over gas burners to keep buffet food hot. He cleaned these meticulously using cold water from the hose and his hands. The moral of this interlude, I decided, was never to eat anything at the museum café!

I stripped and changed my bed linen and got the washing machine going, then did some cleaning. I rang Mr. F. about the phone line. No one had got back to him, he told me, but he would ring them now and find out what was going on. I heard nothing. This did not bode well.

The day progressed. I ventured out to the local supermarket and bought a few odds and ends. The lady in front of me paid for her goods, but there was insufficient change available for her. This is a common occurrence here. There is a shortage of the very small notes and so the prices are rounded up. One wonders why they bother to add the small amounts when there is never any money to cover it. I cannot imagine trying to pay for something in Tesco at £5.19 and accepting that because there wasn't any change, we might as well call it £5.50, or, as in this case, being given some small sweets to the value of the change!

I passed some men loading up supplies for the cruise boats. Today, being Monday, was change-around day, as all the flights came in today. The men had L-shaped boards on their backs, and on to these were loaded crates of drinks; the weight must be enormous. I had noticed the same system for carrying bricks at the building site. I had watched the previous evening as a lorry load of bricks had arrived at about 9:00 p.m., and four teenage boys threw the bricks into a pile beside the road. It took them about half an hour to offload the whole lorry, but I had wondered how many of them had remained in one piece and uncracked after this rather robust method!

In the evening, I decided to go and see Mr. F. in his office and to check on the progress of the phone line. I waded through the mounds of sand and mud, made much more tricky by the dark and the enormous amount of traffic that seemed to have materialised. I think this was due to Ramadan. At 6:00 p.m., the Muslims have "breakfast"; they literally break their fast of the day, and then they all go out to enjoy the worldly pleasures that are not allowed between dawn and dusk during Ramadan. Crossing the road was like trying to cross Hyde Park Corner in rush hour. The additional dust caused by all this traffic was mind blowing and severely hazardous for my contact lenses, which were now unprotected by sunglasses.

I reached the comparative calm of Mr. F.'s office. He gave me the keys for my post office box and told me that the man coming to install the phone line was on two days holiday, but he hoped I would get my phone line very soon now. I hoped so, too. I sat and drank the lemonade brought for me, and he tested me on my Arabic. He was impressed that I had really been trying and gave me some useful phrases to learn: how much, it's possible, it's not possible, go away. I checked the pronunciation with him. The "examination" complete and the elusive phone line discussed, I fought my way home through the dust and traffic.

I was beginning to see a pattern. This morning from the balcony, I had watched a boy and a girl, about ten years old, coming to school together. I had noticed them yesterday, holding hands all the way; they start young here! Here again was the road-sweeping bin man, this morning outside the flats and making a surprisingly good job of his task. Then there was something new. I heard the most terrible din, and when I investigated, I saw a horse and cart laden with calor gas bottles; the driver was hitting the bottle next to him with a spanner. A second man jumped down and lifted off a gas bottle with amazing ease. I could hardly move mine; I had to "walk" it. They stand about 2 feet high, and I couldn't even venture a guess at how much they weigh. He put the gas bottle on one shoulder and set off to the adjacent block of flats. He returned in no time with an obviously empty bottle, which he flung on the cart. They then turned around and were off. Something about the whole scene jogged a memory of my childhood, when the rag and bone man used to come round the streets with his horse and cart, shouting for people to bring things out to him.

The day passed with the inevitable cleaning to keep the ever-present dust at bay. I noticed yet another bruise that came with the much more physical housework here, but the satisfaction is enormous; when there is that amount of dust, the difference one makes wielding a duster and a tin of spray polish is very gratifying.

In the afternoon, I rang for a taxi for another trip to the supermarket. This time the shop was full of many different things. We were approaching the end of Ramadan, when there is a three or four-day feast. I suspected that the super-market was stocking up in preparation. I found all sorts of new things and emerged with three carrier bags. The plas-tic bags here are small, and one needs several for just the minimum of shopping. I cast a thought for Tesco and Boots, where employees now always ask if you need a carrier bag in an effort to save the environment. Are they really going to make any difference to the world at large, I wondered, when here I go through half a dozen bags a day, all of which just get thrown away?

I was then taken to a different fruit seller. We decided between us that the original vendor was something of a crook! My taxi driver, because he thinks the man charges the tourists far too much, and me because this same man tried to give me change for 50 LE when I had given him 100 LE! Fortunately, I was on the ball and argued with him until he gave me the right change. However, on this occasion my taxi driver did all the negotiations. He told me that we would get a better price if he did it. I got a kilo of tomatoes, the same of cucumbers (or they could have been courgettes, I wasn't too sure what I was getting!), a kilo of oranges, and two melons. My bill was 20LEabout £2! Upon returning home, my driver decided that my shopping was not heavy, the inference being that I didn't need help carrying it upstairs. I had always suspected that one lot of assistance was all I was going to get once he knew I lived on the top floor! I agreed that it was fine, and he loaded me up with my carrier bags, chuckling and declaring that now I looked like a real Egyptian woman!

I spent the rest of the day hoping that my phone line was coming, but there was only further disappointment on that front. I rang Mr. F. in the evening, and he said he was trying to contact the man who would be doing the installation. Again, he promised to ring me on my mobile as soon as he had any news. I was now reaching desperation point. I had telephoned the bank in the morning, and my rent money had not gone in from the flat. I rang the estate agent and was told that it might be in my account by the end of next week, but definitely by the end of the month. My finances were looking decidedly "iffy," and my need to get on the Internet to move some money around was becoming paramount. Ah, well, perhaps tomorrow. *Inshalla*!

The days passed in a vague pattern of housework in the early morning, shopping in frequent but small amounts to make the transportation of same easier, sometimes swimming at one of the hotels or walking into different parts of the town for odds and ends with perhaps a coffee stop on the way back. I seemed to be attracting a little less attention now and wondered whether people were beginning to recognise me and leave me alone more.

Sitting on the kitchen balcony with my fruit juice one morning, something caught my eye in the museum courtyard. A man came out of the building and threw something that looked like cauliflower on the ground. He called inside the building, and out came a very large, long-haired brown sheep! I couldn't believe my eyes. Where had that come from, and more to the point, why was it there? Was it a pet, or was it lunch? I wondered how many live sheep were wandering around the kitchens of the British Museum in London! I remembered some English friends telling me that when one of their Egyptian neighbours first moved into their block of flats, a ceremonial goat was brought in and then slaughtered on the doorstep in order to bring good luck, health, and happiness to the new abode. Perhaps there was something of the sort happening at the museum today. Whatever the reason, it was unlikely that I would ever find out.

Daily calls to Mr. F. to check on the progress of the phone line did not seem to be achieving anything. However, returning to the kitchen from my early-morning fruit juice on the balcony, I heard my mobile ringing in the bedroom. It was Mr. F. He had tried me many times, he said. I explained that I had been outside and had not heard the phone. He asked if I could meet his son by the church at 9:30 a.m., as he would take me to the manager of the telephone office and we would push for the phone line to be installed. I looked at my watch: 8:45 a.m. A shower, clothes flung on, lenses put in, breakfast, and I was ready to leave forty minutes later, agonising over whether I should change my T-shirt to something more conservative, but deciding the first choice would have to be fine as I had run out of time.

I arrived at the church spot on at 9:30 a.m., and Mr. F.'s son was there waiting for me. We exchanged the usual pleasantries and started our dice with death down the road to the telephone office. A new hurdle was in our path just outside the office: a puddle so huge it represented the Nile itself, and a vast pile of sand doing a good impression of the Sahara! Mr. F.'s son negotiated a path for me over the "Sahara" and in and out of piles of rubble and wood with large nails sticking out, which were on top of the "dune." However, we arrived in one piece, and I was relieved that I had worn a pair of pumps rather than sandals this time. We entered a different part of the building, which was air-conditioned, and went into the manager's office, Mr. F.'s son first showing his identity card and a letter from his father.

I have found before here in the bank that one can just walk in to the manager's office without knocking and usually without an appointment. That indeed was the case on this particular morning. I was invited to sit down, and the Arabic discourse began. I tried to sit there looking demure—I could imagine my friends' reaction: you, demure?! Nonetheless, I did my best, and whilst I knew the manager spoke excellent English, the Egyptian way was for all the talking to be done on my behalf and for me simply to be in attendance. At the very end of the conversation, I picked out something about tomorrow and maybe Saturday. We left after only twenty minutes—a huge coup in Egyptian time frames—and Mr. F.'s son told me that the phone line would definitely be installed on Saturday and that I could keep the original number.

We parted company, and I walked back along the Nile in the shade and relative cool of the early morning. I enjoyed the walk and was beginning to feel just a tad fitter than when I had arrived. Certainly some of my trousers were fitting better already!

I resurrected the pot of coffee I had had to leave so unceremoniously earlier and sat and read some more of my originally "expensive" newspaper; this paper was beginning to be a good value after all—it had lasted me six days so far! Upon my arrival home, I had discarded my trousers and T-shirt and put on a sarong to cool off. An hour later, my mobile rang. It was Mr. F. He asked if I was at home, because the telephone manager was anxious that I should have my phone line quickly, and the engineer could come straight away. I was thrilled. Quickly I went to the bedroom to replace the sarong with the trousers and T-shirt. I also made a celebratory cup of coffee, keeping my fingers well and truly crossed. Please, let it be right this time.

Five hours later, I rang Mr. F. again. Nobody had come. He informed me that there were only two men dealing with the telephones for the whole of Luxor as it was Ramadan, and if they had not come by 2:00 p.m., they would not come until Saturday, Friday being the Arabic equivalent of the Western Sunday. I was gutted. I had stayed in all afternoon, postponing my trip to the Internet café with my German friend, for nothing. It was 5:10 p.m. I poured myself a huge brandy and Coke, which I dispatched pdq, cried a few tears of shear frustration, and resolved to try the nearby hotel in the morning for an Internet connection.

This proved to be an excellent decision. I bought an hour's Internet time for £4.50 and found that I had 273 emails waiting for me! It took nearly the whole hour to deal with them, and then I was able to address my financial situation, which was a huge relief. However, my rent money had still not reached my account, and some other funds I had been expecting were not there either. I returned home and rang the helpline, inevitably getting a very nice lady in Bombay. She said she would ring me back, which was a relief, as I couldn't imagine how much it was costing me from a mobile. When she rang back, she told me there had been an error and that the funds would be transferred electronically as a priority, but I would not see it in my account until the end of the following week. Clearly I was going to have to be extremely frugal during the week ahead.

The bricks kept coming. I usually heard them being delivered at night, but a new pattern was emerging in the mornings. Four older men built a little wall, then on top of this they loaded a pile of bricks, two at a time, until there were twenty-seven in the pile. This was then secured with a piece of thin rope, and unlike I had previously supposed, a thin slab of cardboard was laid across the man's back and up past his head. He then heaved the twenty-seven bricks onto his back and bent nearly double, hastening into the building. I wondered whether they were paid per load, as there seemed to be some competition between two of the men, who were constantly looking across at each other, comparing their loads. I supposed they got paid a pittance, but it was quite extraordinary the number of bricks that got moved in a relatively short span of time.

I had found some English television. Broadcast between 4:00 p.m. and 8:00 p.m. every day, the channel was called Nile TV. There were a lot of news programmes, but as it was Ramadan, there were a lot of religious programmes, too, which were quite interesting. There was "Islamic Insights" and "Ramadan Glaimpses"—which I presume should have been glimpses! I had also found a soap opera spoken in Arabic with English subtitles. The acting was quite appalling, and the subtitles unintentionally hilarious, but over the course of a few days, it became quite compelling!

The birds were incredible at dusk. I didn't ever remember hearing them before. The noise of them nesting for the night was immense; the only time I had heard the like was in the Northern Territory of Australia. The previous night, I had been sitting on the kitchen balcony and had watched great flocks of them flying in to roost. Perhaps Alfred Hitchcock got his inspiration for the film by sitting in Luxor!

However, the greatest coup of the day was the fact that *my phone line was installed*! I had made my daily call to Mr. F. to chase it up, and he told me that he had been told it would be today, but that if no one had come by 2:00 p.m., I could go out because they did not work after that time. At 10:30 a.m., I was quite resigned to the fact that it wasn't going to happen and decided to take up some curtains which were trailing on the floor. So there I was with my pins and needle and thread, sitting on the floor, hemming. Sewing is another task that I hate with great passion, but on this particular morning it was almost pleasurable—my mother and grandmother would never have believed it! Deep in thought, I nearly jumped out of my skin when the doorbell rang. I opened it cautiously to a rather strange looking, extremely dirty telephone engineer! I couldn't believe it—at last! This man spoke no English whatsoever, and my few words of newly learned Arabic actually came in quite useful. I rang Mr. F., and he spoke to him and then to me in order to translate. The man came in and sat himself down in an armchair and asked for a drink! And I thought BT were bad! Some wires materialised from the balcony, courtesy of his pal downstairs, and they borrowed my stepladder. Then they both came into the flat, looking for old connections. I had to laugh when I recalled Mr. F.'s dire warnings of not letting any men in; he was apparently quite happy for these two to come, and two more dubious looking characters you had yet to see! They wandered into my bedroom, although they did ask first, and to my horror, the first chap leaned over my bed, leaving copious quantities of filthy hand prints on my cream duvet cover! No guessing what my first job was after they left!

The whole procedure took a couple of hours, and then, joy of joys, I had my phone; but more important, I had my Internet connection. I had brought with me a vast selection of phone adapters and found that I needed to use two of them together. I then needed my extension lead for the phone, but after that I was "cooking with gas." The first two dial-up attempts were abortive, and I could feel my blood pressure rising. However, the third attempt from a different phone socket produced the magical noises of dial-up that I so craved. Overjoyed with my success, I checked my emails and tried to send two—ah! I could receive, but I couldn't send. Never mind; I was getting nearer all the time, and I hoped that the friend of Mr. F.' son would be able to iron this out for me before too long. Communication at last!

Sunday is a strange day here. Friday is the Islamic holy day, and the whole of the little town is plunged into an abnormal quietness. However, there is a large Coptic Christian community who celebrate Sunday, but not with the peace of Fridays. Sunday is a busy, bustling day, and I think a market day. I had walked down to the town to post a letter, calling in at the government shop to look at computer desks. I found I could buy just what I needed for about £28. I stopped for a drink and then came back along the Corniche, passing the ferry on the way. It was then that I wondered whether it was market day, for large quantities of people were approaching the ferry with enormous bags of fruit and vegetables. I would think 75 percent of the populace were wearing *galibayas* this morning, Western dress being unusual. The men carried carrier bags in the conventional way, but all the women had their loads on their heads. I was fascinated by how unencumbered they appeared to be, turning their heads from left to right as if there were nothing there. Visions of little old ladies with chins on their chests and no necks at all went through the cinema of my mind and raised a smile. No tennis elbow for any of these ladies—perhaps I should practise!

I spent the rest of the day on the laundry. My first fight was with the washing line, which had got tangled when it was retracted and had tied itself in a knot inside. I self-confess my lack of practicality, and I felt the same way I did when I was first divorced many years ago: frustrated by my own lack of ability and not knowing where to start. I decided to take it all off the wall and peered hopefully inside. After about fifteen minutes, I had found the culprit and somehow managed to untangle it. What a relief! All then went well until my final load, which had some black trousers in it. I thought I had washed them before, but I couldn't have done so. My favourite coffee-coloured towel had become a strange gray-coloured coffee, and the white inset in the black T-shirt was also gray. Similarly, a rather pretty pair of pink knickers which had been in there by mistake had become particularly unsightly! Undaunted, I hung the various items out on the line, deciding to rerun the towel in a hot wash in the hopes that some of the colour would be restored.

This would appear to have been my downfall. The ever-temperamental washing machine picked this moment to leak. 'Twas always thus. Sometimes it's fine; sometimes it isn't; and right now, it wasn't. My washing machine, I decided, epitomises Egyptian workmanship: poor! Then there was the culmination of a particularly onerous afternoon: the bricks. Oh no, not the bricks! My washing still on the line, the usual lorry load of bricks was being delivered, and I dreaded the inevitable cloud of dust it would produce. However, two older men were doing the shift, and whilst they still threw the bricks down, it wasn't with quite the same velocity as the youngsters, and the rising dust was minimal.

Feeling a little depressed by my afternoon, there was only one thing for it: alcohol and a DVD, followed by an early night and a new day in the morning.

November

I was beginning to feel unwell. Thinking it was just reaction to the previous few weeks and anxiety over my financial situation, I decided on a complete day off. I went down to the nearest hotel and settled in for the day. It was delightful. I had a pizza at the poolside restaurant at lunchtime, read a lot, dozed a bit, and peppered it all with dips in the pool. I returned home about 4:00 p.m. feeling relaxed, but with strange sensations in my tummy.

I was awake all night with severe pain. I had experienced this pain before in the UK a couple of times, but despite tests and scans, it remained a mystery. This had been my biggest fear—that this mystery pain would strike me in Egypt. Trying to stay calm, I took the cocktail of painkillers that I had been prescribed before and spent the day in bed.

Thus followed the next three days. On the third day I began to wonder if this was a kidney infection, so I decided on a course of antibiotics my lovely UK G.P. had prescribed for the trip. I had not anticipated needing them this soon! I decided I would give these a couple of days, and if I was no better, I would have to ask Mr. F. for the doctor.

By the next day I was beginning to feel more human, and the day after that I was much more myself. I was beginning to feel more positive about everything, and I realised that my slip into gloom had been part of my ill health.

During my malaise, I had become quite obsessed with the goings-on in the museum café kitchen. There was a definite turn round of staff, with one set being in uniform—smart terracotta jackets. Ramadan now over, the prayer mat had been relegated to the back courtyard, along with the small mobile "altar" that had been placed in front of it. In its place in the middle of the courtyard were three large pot plants. It seemed a strange place to put them, all things considered! A small battalion of cats and kittens seemed suddenly to have taken residence at the museum. They wandered about both day and night.

There was a bath-like apparatus masquerading as a sink, and on the opposite side, tables were put together with containers for the cutlery. I watched people wash the dishes by dipping a sponge into a bucket of soapy water—just the sponge, not the dish—and then rinse the dish under a running tap. The dishes were then piled up, upside down, in huge piles. Another boy then came with a tea towel the size of a bath towel and dried them. This towel was used to dry everything—dishes, hands, and faces. Earlier I had watched him polish his shoes with a pink towel and was just waiting for him to dry the dishes with it, too, but if he actually did so, I never saw him! I felt the inclination to hang a big sign from my balcony warning people not to eat there, but I dare say even the smart hotel kitchens are very similar, and what the eye doesn't see, the heart doesn't grieve over. But I was beginning to realise why so many people have bad tummies when visiting Egypt!

My own routine at home in Egypt was based on hygiene and was so very different from the mindset in the UK where things don't get covered in dust within moments of cleaning them, or insects that materialize in seconds if something is dropped. I always started the morning, whilst still in my nightie, by cleaning the kitchen surfaces with a Dettol spray. Only after three weeks was I beginning to get on top of the dust that way. The rest of the kitchen and bathroom I also cleaned daily. I was meticulous about sweeping up crumbs and spills instantly to avoid the ever-present armies of ants. These ants were enormous, probably as big as a small house spider in England. My German friend told me to put vinegar in the water when I washed the floors to keep the ants under control, and I had been doing it religiously ever since.

Similarly, I never left washing up to dry or piles of washing that needed doing. There were a huge amount of flies here; I was being eaten alive the first ten days I arrived. I always checked cups and mugs and gave them a wipe before using them because of the dust. My thoughts flew to my younger daughter in Australia, who told me stories of battling large, nasty spiders in the house and snakes in the garden. My problems here were less hazardous, but it did promote a different way of thinking.

After most of the week feeling unwell, my provisions were virtually nil, so off to the supermarket I went. This time I had the forethought to take my computer backpack with me to pack the shopping in, thus saving the tennis elbow. First I went to Plastic Alley to check the computer desk situation and to buy a bucket and a washing up bowl. The kitchen sink is enormous and takes a lot of water to fill. The water is metered, so this is not the best idea. Added to which, the plugs tend to leak, and if you left anything to soak, it left a dreadful ring round the sink that took weeks to get rid of. I set off with great motivation, only to trip on one of the mats at the bottom of the marble stairs and fall in most unladylike fashion across them. A very nice man from the shop helped me up, and when I came back down again, stood at the bottom, pointing out the mat! No Health and Safety regulations here! When I had arrived the shop was empty, but by the time I went to pay there was a crowd round the till. I waited in good British fashion for a while and then decided on the Egyptian option. I pushed my way to the front, dumped my purchases on the desk and got out my purse. The effect was amazing, and I was soon leaving the shop. I must remember not to do this in Tesco when I return!

I went to the supermarket to stock up and then to the fruit and vegetable man. While I was there, my driver loaded up my backpack for me. We returned home, and he helped me with the backpack. I couldn't believe the weight of it! He handed me my bucket and washing up bowl with the fruit and vegetables in it and thrust into my other hand the remaining carrier bag, which he told me was not heavy! With the words "good Egyptian woman" ringing in my ears, I slowly, very slowly, climbed the four flights to my front door!

The previous evening I had gone to visit Mr. F. at his office. It was the first day he had been there after the feasting following Ramadan. The roads round the main square and round the square near his office were completely demolished, but still heavily trafficked. I watched a taxi rolling its way over the bumps and gravel and dust and wondered what it was doing to the axle. My driver had told me that it was very good for business because nobody wanted to walk! This I could understand. The Egyptian traffic was always a nightmare, but round these squares it was positively suicidal. With the added dust, it became quite fog-like, and to a contact lens wearer, nothing could be worse. I relentlessly ploughed on, doing 50 percent of the journey with my eyes closed every time something particularly large or fast passed, creating an extra surge in the dust cloud.

I reached the office with some relief and found a queue. I sat down and waited. To my embarrassment, I was ushered in ahead of the other people waiting and greeted warmly. Five minutes later, we were joined by an Egyptian girl and her young son of about seven or eight. The youngster remained in the outer office with the secretary, watching television. Mr. F. divided his time between the two of us, switching from Arabic to English with barely a thought. He tested me on the days of the week in Arabic, and we went through my inevitable list of things. He sent his secretary off to buy me a phone card to enable me to make international calls, and the Egyptian girl sent her little boy off to the bakery to buy me some rolls that I had been unable to find. As I was still having troubles with my email, Mr. F. rang his son and told me that he and his friend would be round tomorrow at 5:00 p.m. to see if they could fix the problem for me. I asked about the computer desk; if I were to buy it, how would I get it home? Mr. F. thought about this for a moment or two and then declared that we would employ the services of the lad who always carried the bags up the stairs to the flat on my arrival, as he had a car. I was astounded. However, I had misheard, and seeing my amazement, he qualified the statement by saying that he had a donkey and cart—I had not heard the original T! After about an hour, feeling that I was stopping him from working despite his protestations that this was not so, I returned home.

Mr. F.'s son and his friend arrived shortly after 5:00 p.m. the following day. There were enormous problems with the Internet that day, and they told me that this was often the case in Luxor. However, he acknowledged how painfully slow everything was and proclaimed it a problem with the phone line, not my computer. He suggested a DSL line, which would be many times faster, and said I would only pay a monthly charge regardless of how long I was online. "Ah, like broadband?" I enquired hopefully.

"No," they chorused, "not like Broadband."

However, they could split the line so that I could use the phone at the same time and get me a wireless router, which would also help. Needless to say, this was all going to cost more money, but the frustration of the current situation made it an easy decision. They left to get everything ordered for me, telling me they hoped everything would be taken care of within the week. Ah, yes, but I had heard this before!

It was suddenly noticeably cooler in the early mornings and evenings. It was only sixty-eight degrees on the balcony at 6:30 a.m., a good four degrees cooler than earlier mornings. In the evenings I was turning the air-conditioning off because it was getting a bit too cool by 8:30 p.m. I noticed this particular morning that a few leaves were just beginning to fall off the trees. I ventured forth for my first check of the mailbox. I almost remembered the way, but had to ask at the last turning. The man in the post box office was asleep on his desk. He raised himself as I went in and checked my number and let me open the box. My anticipation was short-lived, as my box was empty, despite the fact that I was expecting a couple of things from the UK. I wondered how long they would take. I had been to the post office counter that morning to buy stamps and asked for a special stamp for a letter that had to arrive as fast as possible. I was told the cost was exactly the same! Knowing that a letter I had written to my daughter in my first week had still not arrived, I wondered just how long this post was going to take. My guess was two or three weeks on average.

The following morning, I decided to go farther afield and walk to one of the hotels at the opposite side of town. It took me forty minutes to get there, and it seemed a long way. I was walking on what I thought was the shady side of the road, but on the last third of the walk there was no shade on either side of the road. The Egyptians never use the pavements, but always walk in the road, and this morning they were walking in the middle of the road. I didn't wonder why for long—this was the only shady part. However, I decided that I would rather walk in the sun than dice with death in the middle of the road! The pavements are a hazard by themselves, the kerbs being twelve to eighteen inches high and interspersed with huge gaps, so that one is permanently climbing up and down them. This is probably why the local people refrain from using them.

I reached my destination and sat in the coffee shop drinking coffee. I was brought two sachets of Nescafe and a huge teapot of boiling water that would have made a minimum of six cups! Two complimentary chocolates accompanied it. Egyptian chocolates always look amazing but taste rather like ex-lax! On this occasion, they were peanuts covered in dark chocolate. It was so long since I had eaten any chocolate that I found they actually tasted wonderful! I couldn't decide whether they really did taste good, or whether it was just my deprivation of confectionery of any kind that made the difference.

I wandered round the hotel shops and then popped into the hotel next door and had a look at the shops there. I decided I had better top up my fluid levels before the long walk home, so I sat and had a cold drink there. By now it was midday—a silly time to undertake a long walk in the sun. Echoes of my mother rang in my ears—goodness how her words haunted me here! I had spent childhood holidays in the Mediterranean sun, where my fair complexion was always a problem.

However, I set out at a leisurely pace, crossing the road when necessary to stay in the shade, and got back in another forty minutes. Along the way I had watched a team of men taking basket-like crates of fruit and vegetables onto the various cruise ships, today being turnaround day again. Then a little further along armies of tourists were coming off the buses and walking along the quay to their cruise boats, some of which were moored seven abreast. I was beginning to enjoy being a resident and watching the regular comings and goings of the tourists. I actually enjoyed the walk, although I was very tired and thirsty on my return.

Once home, I logged on again to see if my rent money had come in, but no. There was an email from the agent saying she would look into this for me, but alas, she had said this last week, too. No reply either from the travel agent handling the forthcoming conference I was involved with to confirm that they were going to get me back to Luxor at the end of the ten days. I telephoned in desperation and was told someone would phone me back shortly, but I was still waiting!

I was beginning to feel in need of a haircut. I checked back in my diary. Yes, I thought so; it was six weeks since I had previously had it cut. I thought I could probably get away with another couple of weeks, but then I would have to make the decision as to who would give me the cut, and where. My German friend told me that a European woman owned the hairdressers at three of the large hotels, and she thought they all had good reputations. Mr. F. had said he would ask his wife, but I had not heard anything, and as he did so much for me, I didn't like to ask him again. I thought I would probably choose the nearest hotel to where I lived. This was going to be a scary prospect! Would I have to attend the forthcoming conference with a paper bag over my head?!

I spent another evening with Mr. F., and I had directions to the nearest bakery. I set out the next morning, not at all sure where I was going. However, his instructions were good, and I found it without too much difficulty. Bakery was rather a grand title for the open shop I found with trestle tables in front of it. The bread and rolls were laid out on the tables and covered with polythene. A young boy served me. He picked up my first request with his hand in an inverted plastic bag, but by the time I got to my third buy, he was just picking the bread up in his fingers! I set off again, chuffed that I had found it and actually bought what I had needed.

I went home via a different road to find an electrical shop. I had been here before to buy a bedside light and was looking now for a lamp for the sitting room. I found the shop and went in. They had a limited selection, but what they had was very nice. I saw a couple of things I liked and decided on one at the grand cost of £25. I couldn't buy it there and then, as I would have needed both hands to carry it home and I already had the bread and also some milk, but I resolved to go back another day.

On my return home, there was good news and bad waiting for me. The good news was that my rent money had materialised and the travel agent had confirmed that they would arrange for my return to Luxor at the end of the conference. The bad news was the water. When I had got back from Mr. F.'s office the previous night, there was hardly any water. All the time I had been here, the pump downstairs had been making a funny noise and was only coming on intermittently. It hadn't been running at all the night before. Unsure of whether this was indeed a pump problem or whether the water was just off for a few hours, which happens occasionally, I had left it for a while. By 5:00 p.m., I decided I had a problem and rang the long-suffering Mr. F. By 6:45 p.m. he had sent his son round with an electrician. It was indeed the pump: the motor had burned out. The electrician needed 20 LE to go and buy a replacement, and by 8:00 p.m. and another £2 tip, I had an excellent stream of water coming from all my taps. What a relief. The day had been something of a challenge, washing my hands in bottled water, not washing up or flushing the loo. It is a continuous source of amazement that workmen come out in the evenings and that the shops are open for the various parts needed. However, call for them in the afternoon and it is a lost cause, as they are all asleep!

The next morning, I opened the curtains to find a cloudy sky and quite a breeze. It was a pleasant change and nice to open the windows and feel some air, albeit dusty air! I resolved to spend a quiet day reading and doing a little housework. I opened my emails, and one of them necessitated a phone call to my friend in England. We spoke for some time, but mid-sentence my credit ran out on the phone and we were cut off. So much for my quiet morning at home!

I walked down to the nearest shop for a top-up card and then went on to the telecom's office to get another card for my landline. This card enabled me to make international calls from my landline. It took me three attempts to get it. Each time I was referred on to a different office in a different part of the building. Patience not being one of my virtues, I could feel my tolerance level diminishing. Before I became too irritable, I asked one of the security guards. He took me personally to the office and showed me a bank of telephones. No, no, I did not need to make a call; I just needed the card. Eventually he understood and took me to the counter and explained what I needed. My purchase was hastily made. At least I would know exactly where I was going the next time.

In the midst of all this, I had received a call from my tenant in the UK who was having problems with the heating. It seemed strange that she was experiencing the first frost of winter when I was feeling decidedly hot and sweaty! We discussed what she should do next, and I could only keep my fingers crossed that it wasn't going to cost too much money to remedy.

I went home via the ATM, as I had previously seen a notice saying they accepted Maestro cards. This was most unusual, as I had never been able to use my NatWest card here before. I wasn't overly confident, but decided that if I used it during banking hours, at least if it swallowed up my card,

I could go into the bank and hopefully get it retrieved. With bated breath, I put the card into the slot. To my amazement and joy, the machine dispensed my money. This was going to be a huge boon and would help matters no end.

With a new spring in my step, I went down a side street to go home via the shop for more milk. It was now approaching midday when the whole of Luxor seem to be on the road. The traffic situation is not helped by the fact that the local "buses" are in fact people carriers. You can stop one in the street at any point and get off where you want for a minimal amount of money (twenty-five piastres—about 2.5p). This, of course, causes complete havoc, as the drivers stop on a sixpence if they think they have another fare, and everybody just has to wait until they set off again, amidst much hooting and tooting. These vehicles were now nose to tail, and I wondered how on earth I was going to cross the road. At that moment, a young Egyptian boy approached me and asked what I was looking for, saying he would help me. There is nothing like this sort of hassle to make one risk crossing the road as the locals do. In my anxiety to escape being "helped," I just stepped out into the road, a prayer hovering on my lips for safe delivery to the other side. I emerged unscathed and amazed on the opposite side!

However, I rather wished I hadn't bothered, as the shop was completely out of milk. I had, yet again, to take my chances crossing back. This afternoon I had planned to make a dessert, but without the milk it would have to wait for another day. I had bought a packet of "chocolate custard," mainly because I found the translation so terribly funny. It read as follows:

"Holw el Sham Custard. Chocolate. Best Taste in No Time

Preparation methods:

Dissolve all the content of packed to kilo of cold milk and make it sweetness with sugar as desired. To setit on moderate fire with continuous stirring till achievement of the preferred consistency. Pour immediately upon lifting it from the fire. Lift for cooling and then put in the refrigerator."

I think it was the "setit on moderate fire" that did it for me; I just couldn't leave it on the shelf after that. However, the joys of "Holw el Sham" would have to wait for another day.

That evening saw my first "girls' night out." I was invited to join my German friend and another English friend of hers who lived on her block. I rang my driver and booked his taxi for 7:15 p.m. There was a misunderstanding over the time, and he arrived at 7:30 p.m. I got to my friend's flat ten minutes late, and we collected my fellow countrywoman and set off. We walked the first part, as there were things to do on the way. At 8:00 p.m. the main street was heaving with people and traffic, and it was too far for the little legs of my German friend's two-year-old son, so we got a taxi and went on to the restaurant. We had a very good meal for about £3.50, including tip and drinks, then walked further up the road to a balcony café where we could observe the comings and goings whilst having a drink. When we asked for the bill, the very young waiter asked "and for tips?" My English companion was horrified and immediately told the owner, whom she knew very well. The youngster was instructed not to ask for tips, and we were told it was his first day. However, by the time we reached the pavement and were getting in a taxi, the same boy appeared to tell us that he had lost his job. It was a harsh lesson for him to learn. The three of us shared a taxi, which dropped us off in three different locations; my friend and her little boy at home, the other English lady at another location where she was meeting someone, and myself back home. We went from one end of town to the other, with three stops, for a total of £2 including tip.

The next morning, I decided, must be the one for household chores. I spent the whole morning on half the flat, resolving to finish later in the afternoon when the sun was on the wane. The day before I had been bitten all over my left arm, probably from where I had leaned on something that had objected! The worst bites were all round my elbow, the same side as the tennis elbow. This made it difficult to rub in the anti-inflammatory gel that had been helping. As I got started into the day, the pain became so debilitating that I thought I might have to seek someone who could inject some steroids for me before very much longer. Perhaps the enforced lack of physical and computer use during the ten days of the conference might make a difference.

At lunchtime I sat at the computer and was immediately accosted by a solitary fly. How it got in I could never understand, as the windows all had mosquito grills across them, but there was always one that makes it in! I had covered myself in an aerosol spray for sting relief, which had taken my breath away. Now, infuriated by the fly, I gently picked up the can of fly-killer on the table beside me and squirted it remorselessly. Sitting in a cloud of asphyxiating fumes, I wondered who would go first, the fly or me! However, although I had never seen it go or heard it die, the fly-killer seemed to have done the trick, and my own lungs still seemed to be functioning!

I had a snack lunch and investigated the heat on the balcony, which was next on my cleaning list. It was still far too hot. It was a good moment to put on the Pilates DVD and try to get a little fitter. I did the warm up exercises and decided that was quite sufficient for a first go! Feeling my age and then some, I completed my cleaning and turned my efforts to those of a culinary sort. I had brought with me some of my favourite vegetarian recipes, but there always seemed to be one or two ingredients I couldn't get. In an enthusiastic moment of compromise, I turned out a wonderful variation on a sweet potato stew, inadvertently making enough to feed a family of six! However, several portions stacked away in the freezer gave a satisfactory outcome, and I settled in with a huge plateful and a DVD.

I woke very early the next morning; without the need for air-conditioning, I had left the window open, and the call to prayer at 5:00 a.m. disturbed me. I was as stiff as a plank! I didn't know whether it was the enthusiastic cleaning or the Pilates exercises that had done it. I creaked my way into the kitchen for the morning fruit juice and put a load of washing on.

At 10:00 a.m. the taxi came to collect me for a big shopping expedition. As he turned the car around, he laughed and said something about babies. I turned to see what he was looking at and saw three little boys about eight years old, sitting in a row on the kerbstones and smoking cigarettes! I was horrified, but he thought it was funny. He then told me how he had seen a woman in the street in Luxor, dressed only in a bikini. He was outraged; he had never seen anything like it.

"In the street," he kept telling me, adding, "Bikini, very small!"

I could see how this would offend the community here, and I wondered at the insensitivity of some people. Sadly, the lady concerned had been English. I had been fairly amazed when sitting in a hotel the previous week; I'd seen a couple walk across the lobby, which incorporated several different coffee shops, restaurants, and shops, clearly coming straight from the pool. The lady was in shorts and a very skimpy top, but the man was only in very tight swimming trunks. It was so inappropriate here and stuck out like a sore thumb. Regrettably, this couple looked as though they also could have been English.

Our first stop on the shopping spree was to the government shop and, although I had been there many times, noticed now with interest called itself "Habitat"! I bought a small table there, which I'd had my eye on for a couple of weeks, my intention being to put a lamp on it and illuminate a dark corner. It was a small round table, painted gold, and very Egyptian looking. It cost £4.50. Next I went to Plastic Alley to buy my computer desk. While I was there, I replaced my saucepan with the broken handle and also picked up a sieve. Next came a garlic press, as the existing one had fallen apart, and a new can opener, as I had cut myself on a tin earlier this week by fighting to open it with a can opener that just wasn't man enough for the job. I chose my computer desk, which they reduced to £25 from £27.50—not because I had asked them to, but I think because I qualified as a big spender! I paid and left it there for the man with his donkey and cart to collect for me.

I went home via a fruit shop. I bought far more than I intended because the man kept peeling fruit for me to try. I bought something I had never seen before that tasted wonderful. It was similar in size and colour to a tomato, but with the texture of a plum. They laughed when I bought some, as they said it was good for men and worked like Viagra! I then returned to await delivery of the desk, and my driver said he would collect me in the afternoon to do the supermarket shopping.

On my way upstairs, I met a neighbour from two floors down. She was a lovely lady in long, flowing robes. She spoke very little English. She invited me in, but sadly, I had to refuse as I was awaiting my delivery. I hoped she would repeat the invitation another time. Her door was open, and her flat looked very plush and lovely. She seemed to know exactly who I was and was quite delightful.

The computer desk arrived at noon, and I laughed at myself for the amount of pleasure it afforded. It was lovely to get things organised and to release the dining room table. At last I could type at a comfortable angle, and everything looked neat and tidy. Success!

Sundays, I decided, would be my post box day. I trundled my way down to the post office and checked the box— two letters and a postcard, how exciting! As much as I was pleased to receive mail, I was also relieved that it was reaching me. I regret that I hadn't shared the Egyptian confidence in this respect. I tucked the post in my basket and made my way back to the lamp shop.

On the way back down a little alley, I passed a dozen or more flat breads laid carefully on round stones, just lying in the street to dry in the hot sun before baking. An odd fly or two landed on them, and I wondered whether this was the way the flat breads I had been buying were also cooked. It crossed my mind that this was exactly the way this type of bread has been prepared since Pharaohnic times, as indeed one sees the peasants toiling in the fields, scattering seeds by hand, and ploughing with oxen, without any real changes over the millennia.

I reached the lamp shop, which was unexpectedly closed. I presumed the owner must be a Christian, as the majority of shops and offices are open on Sundays. Deciding on a change of plan for the rest of the day, I resolved to have my hair cut in the afternoon rather than the following day. Then I returned home to read my post.

One of the letters was the tenancy agreement for my UK flat, needing a witnessed signature. I read it studiously and was interested to see that the tenant undertook to pay interest if the rent was late. As I had waited nearly a month for my first payment, I rattled off a letter to the agent, claiming my compensation, and emailed it, putting the hard copy with the agreement. I would take it down to Mr. F. later and ask him to witness my signature.

At 2:30 p.m., I went down to the hotel to brave the hairdressers' scissors. A carpet shop man told me they were closed for lunch. He insisted I go into his shop for a cup of tea and a chat to pass the time. This young man had been studying Egyptian history at Leeds University. We chatted for about a quarter of an hour and had a cup of tea, by which time the hairdressers were open. I bade him farewell and thanked him for the tea, declining his invitation to become his "close friend" because I was a "very beautiful woman"!

The hairdresser was a pleasant young man. I showed him the photographs that I had had taken in the UK after a haircut, and he nodded diligently. He then set about the task as if he was in some kind of race, taking phone calls and sorting out problems in the middle of it and returning to the scissors with a frenzied approach. When I thought of the care and attention my hairdresser of some twenty years took over my hair in England, I hardly dared to look. Also, he didn't appear to be cutting very much off at all, and I was beginning to think I would have to find an alternative in another couple of weeks. He finished the cut and started to blow dry, scalding me several times over and dangling the flex of the hairdryer across my face so that it kept hitting my nose. I was now feeling completely distraught about the final outcome. After he had dried it, he set about styling it with hairspray. I looked at the can, which said "Lacca–very strong"! He sprayed several strands of hair, holding the can almost close enough to touch them, until they were wet again. Then he ran the comb through, achieving exactly the look he had seen in my photo, except *that* had been achieved with the tiniest amount of hair wax. This continued around my whole head, and then for good measure, he sprayed the whole thing again. Memories of the fly spray were conjured up. No wonder I had a cough—my poor lungs were being attacked by aerosols and dust! With the true pride of an artist, he stood back and surveyed the results, asking, "good, eh?" I squinted a terrified look, but to my amazement, the overall effect was excellent and not far removed from what I was trying to achieve. I gave him a tip, and he kissed the money; it was only 70p, which was all the small change I had, but clearly he was pleased with it. I tried to explain that I would be in Luxor till May and would be coming back, but it took three of us to make it clear, as no one in the shop spoke very much English.

Then came the interesting bit! I walked out of the hotel feeling rather pleased and took my sunglasses out. Ah! My hair was so rigid that I couldn't get the arms of the sunglasses through the hair to reach my ears! I touched it. It was like concrete! No worry about walking back in the strong breeze then; this hairstyle would be with me for a fortnight if I needed it to be!! Neither could I get the sunglasses in under the hair—it was unrelenting! I battled on for a bit longer and eventually managed to get the sunglasses within a few centimeters of my ears, which was going to have to do.

The next morning I looked in the mirror with interest. My head had made a sort of crunching sound as it hit the pillow the night before, and rather as I had expected, my hair looked completely untouched. I wondered if I would ever get a hairbrush through it, but with a little perseverance, I managed to brush some of it.

After breakfast I went back to the lamp shop. I bought the lamp, a light bulb, and an extension lead for my computer so that I could plug both it and the printer in together. However, on returning home I found that the adapters would not accommodate the three-pin English plugs. Also, for some extraordinary reason, the Egyptian plug would not fit in the socket. I tried it in other sockets; it fitted some and not others, but I could not understand why. It looked as though I would have to go back to the shop, but it could wait until tomorrow.

I went back down to the government shop via the post box to post a letter. I still needed an extra pillow. I went in and enquired to which a woman responded, "No, after tomorrow." I told her that she had said that last week, and she roared with laughter and said that they were "finished now." Undeterred, I decided to try another smaller government shop.

I went on a roundabout route and stopped for a coffee. When I got to the second shop, I stepped past the same man sitting on the step as I had encountered the first time, except that he was awake. I asked for a pillow. After a lot of discussion and enquiry as to whether I was living in Luxor, a woman called a young lad and told me that he would take me to buy the pillow. We walked all round the back streets, which was fascinating, and then stopped at a shop where we picked up a youngster who took us down another alley. Here a man made a big show of unlocking his shop front— but despite the huge padlocks, none of them were actually locked! He beckoned me in and went upstairs. My original "guide" bade me sit down, ceremoniously wiping the chair for me. Clouds of dust rose from it, and I wondered just what state my trousers would be in after I got up. However, sit I did. I declined the usual cup of tea, and to my amazement, the shop owner reappeared downstairs with some material and sat down at an ancient sewing machine, whereupon he proceeded to make a pillow for me. He folded the length of cotton in half and stitched the two sides, then stuffed it with a cross between fibreglass and cotton wool! Finally, he stitched the end and charged me £4. My companion took me back to his shop, as by then I was totally lost and disorientated, and I gave him 50p for taking me.

It was now lunchtime, so I made a light lunch and tried the chocolate custard I had managed to make the day before. I touched it with the spoon and thought perhaps Tim Henman could make better use of it! As the packet had referred to a kilo of milk, I had taken a guess at the amount and obviously got it wrong. I had used a pint, and I think it should have been a litre. However, the taste was acceptable, reminding me rather of blancmange.

I was restless that night. The cold I'd feared was brewing had never materialised; instead, an unrelenting, dry cough had developed and was always worse the moment I lay down. Every muscle round my rib cage hurt, and my throat was horribly sore. The linctus I had brought from the UK was for chesty coughs and had made no difference at all, so I went into the pharmacy at the end of my road. I stood in good, orderly, British fashion behind two Egyptian ladies but was immediately served by a young man behind the counter. I explained that I had a "tight" cough, and he disappeared, re-emerging with a bottle in one hand and an instruction leaflet in the other, which he gave me. It appeared to control every symptom I had, so he put it in a plastic bag for me and I went on to the electrical shop.

Here I explained to the man that the pins were too big to fit into the socket, and he nodded, as if to say, "and your point is?"

His colleague, who was chatting on a mobile phone, reached into a bin and pulled out an adaptor. This, I was told, would solve the problem (which appeared to be quite commonplace). I took it home and tried. It was perfect. My English adaptors fit into the sockets, and the Egyptian adaptors fit into the wall sockets, so I was set. My computer and printer were now plugged in to English adaptors in an extension lead, which was then plugged into an Egyptian adaptor and into the socket! I laughed as I thought of the hundreds of pounds I had had to spend to get the electrics at my UK flat certified as safe. The electrical systems in Egypt were probably lethal, but everybody lived with it. The ceiling lights dangled precariously and you could see all the wires, the air-conditioning kept blowing the fuse, and the lights came on and off depending on the varying current, and everything worked on a system of adaptors!

Of course, this sort of haphazard approach is very typically Egyptian and applies to just about everything, and yet the majority of the population had mobile phones, and although home computers were rare, the Internet cafés were always packed and most people were computer literate. It was a strange mixture of skills and technical ability.

I went for a walk along the Corniche and heard something that gladdened my heart. Along with the usual cries of "taxi, lady?" or "caleche?" or "you want a felucca?" I also heard, "not tourist, local." Yes! It had taken a month, but somebody had realised that I was living here! I wondered if it would take the remaining six months before most people recognised me and whether I would have to go through the whole painful process again next time I came.

Mr. F. had told me the Arabic for "go away," and I used it to great effect, especially with the children. I told him how successful it was, and he laughed and said yes, if I said that, everyone would go away. I wondered exactly what it was he had told me to say! It seemed cruel to ignore the children, when all they wanted was a little money, sweets, or pens, but if you gave to one, you immediately found you had an ever-increasing crowd around you wanting the same. If you were with a local Egyptian when it happened, he or she got very cross and sent them away immediately. They were difficult to send away, as most of them were beautiful, with dark, dark eyes, and equally dark, softly curling hair. They were always so friendly and very polite:

"Hello, Madame, do you have a little something for me?"

As I had walked passed the school that morning, a huge crowd of little faces peered through the gate, looking as though they were in prison, but every face was smiling. They just wanted to see what was going on outside. Every morning when they got to school, they sang and chanted. Apparently they were singing that they love their school, and it certainly did appear that way.

15.12.2006 11:07

Basket shopping from the balcony

Flowering tree

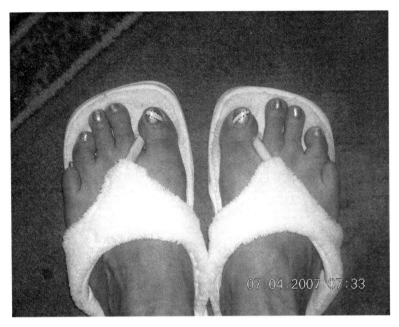

Painted toes Egyptian style

Sheep in Museum Kitchen

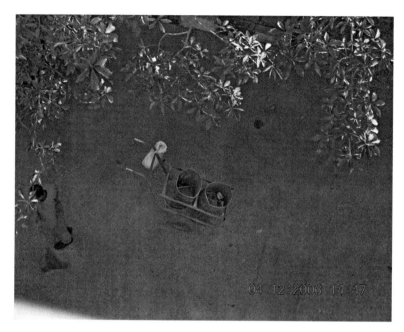

The Bin Man

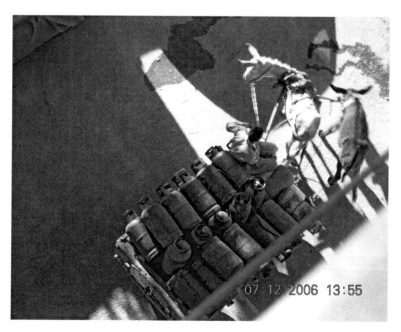

The Bottled Gas Man

Tree cutting

Walk over the mountain

December

I was beginning to understand the rudiments of shopping here. You could get some of the things some of the time, but you could never get all of the things you needed all of the time. There was a local supermarket close to the flat, but it hardly ever had anything in it. I was beginning to know the man behind the till quite well. He spoke perfect English, and I wondered if he was a guide and working at the supermarket to supplement his income, as I knew some of them did. On this occasion I found flour, which I'd been looking for for weeks. I picked up a bag, then found some frozen carrots. The fresh carrots seemed to be in short supply, so this was a good find. I added some frozen ochra, a tub of halva, and two litre-bottles of Diet Coke.

I stood at the till behind two elderly Egyptian Muslim women, their skin wizened and wrinkled. They were going over and over the things in their baskets with the man at the checkout, and I wondered if they didn't have enough money. As the thought crossed my mind, I realised that I didn't have a lot of cash on me, either. I did a quick count and found I had £4. Anxious not to go through a fiasco similar to the two elderly ladies, I left my basket on the floor and put the ochra back in the freezer; that had been an impulse buy, and I still had some at home, but the rest I needed. I waited. An elderly gentleman walked straight past us all and put his shopping on the counter. To my amazement, the man behind the till indicated to him that I was next—this was a first! He looked up at me with a grin and said,

"Sorry about this."

He checked my shopping through the till—it came to £2—and I left, leaving the two elderly ladies still at it!

Along the way back home was a man with a barrow. He had on it something that looked like cherries, except they were green. I recognised them, but couldn't place them.

I looked at the end of the barrow, where he had coffee to drink; ah, of course, coffee beans in their entirety.

My chest having been wracked the previous night by my cough, I called back into the pharmacy. The man recognised me and smiled. I said I still had the bad cough, and now I had a streaming cold. Before I could ask for what I thought I wanted, a pharmacist said that she had something very good for this and disappeared to the back of the shop. She came back with some Panadol Cold and Flu Tablets. I asked if I could take them with the cough linctus, and she said I could, so I requested another bottle. She then asked if I was taking antibiotics, to which I replied no.

"No?!" She appeared horrified.

She was sure my cough would never get better without antibiotics. I was inclined to agree. I had a cupboard full of pills and potions, but after nearly a week, I was feeling just the same; in fact, I think I felt worse. She pulled down some Augmentin and decided I only needed the small dose. I paid and went home. When I went to take my round of pills, I found that I had only been shown the dosage instructions, but not given them, and she had given me so much information that I couldn't remember what to do. The Augmentin was labeled, but the Panadol was not, so I decided to err on the side of caution rather than overdose. The cough linctus was slightly different than what I'd used before, and there were no instructions at all, so I would have to use my common sense. Hopefully, as I rattled through the rest of the day, my chest would release its mighty grip with the help of at least one of these potions!

I unpacked the shopping and wiped it all. I had gone to great lengths to pick a packet of flour without a hole—my hands becoming totally white in the process—but as I picked the packet up to wipe, a little cloud of white flour emerged from a hole I had not noticed!

I decided to make carrot and lentil soup for lunch. It was a huge success, and I put some away in the freezer for future use. I had also bought a packet of chocolate ice cream mix. It included the usual approximate guide for quantities, with phrases such as, "take one glass of milk." What size glass exactly would that be? I got the mixer out of the cupboard. This was something that Mr. F. had bought on my behalf when he first stocked the flat for me, and I was unsure at the time that I would ever use it, thinking I would only ever be here for a week's holiday. How pleased I was to have it now. I followed the instructions and ended up with something that looked as though it could pass as ice cream. I put it in the freezer with my fingers crossed.

The previous afternoon, I had decided to take a little stroll in the opposite direction from the town, towards Karnak. The afternoon was cooler than usual, and it was pleasant to walk along beside the boats and watch the river. There was less hassle walking in this direction, as the main tourist attractions were back the other way. It was a nice change to amble along, left alone for the most part. I stopped and watched a cruise boat that looked as if it was about to leave, but in fact it was still there on my way back. Farther along, I stopped and looked across the river. To my amazement, I found I was directly opposite Hatchetsup's Temple, which I could see quite clearly in the distance. There was something rather timeless in the experience as I realised that this particular vista must be totally unchanged from when this temple had first been built. There was nothing there except the river with palm trees and vegetation close to its banks, the sandy mountains and the desert beyond, and the temple nestling into the clefts of the mountain. I felt for those few moments as if I were in a little time bubble; it was a moment to treasure.

I turned back and walked towards home. I had not much further to go when a man approached me and told me where the market was. I ignored him. He persisted. Finally, I turned to him and told him that I was not a tourist, but that I lived here. The reaction was better than any I could possibly have hoped for. With a loud exclamation of, "Omigod! Have a nice afternoon," he actually ran off!

I was amazed. I decided to try the same thing again when someone asked if I wanted a felucca just as I was about to cross the road for home. This time, there was a mouthful of Arabic that I didn't understand, but the end result was the same: no more hassle. I resolved to use this more often in the future.

The bricks had definitely stopped coming to the building site opposite my flat, and the pile of sand that had replaced them was slowly diminishing. The first morning I had looked out, a man was filling a large, heavy-duty paper bag with the sand using his hands. He then heaved it onto his shoulder with obvious difficulty and carried it across the road to where they were mixing concrete. However, the following day I was relieved to see that they had obtained a wheelbarrow. Although there had been much activity all the time I had been here, I couldn't actually see anything different at all about the building itself, and I wondered how long it was going to take to complete.

I had made a timing mistake when I went to the pharmacy. I had left home just before noon, and it seemed that the school children had finished a little early that day. Added to that was the arrival of a "real" dustcart—a lorry, something I had never seen here before—that was a source of immense interest. Clearly the children hadn't seen this often, either. There must have been one hundred children milling round the lorry and spilling out right across the road. Some of the children were very small. They wore khaki-coloured uniforms of trousers and long tunic-like jackets with long sleeves. Some of the little girls had skirts, but most were in trousers. Most of them had rucksacks on their backs, and all of them, without exception, were terribly friendly and keen to talk. Needless to say, none of them saw any necessity to move so that I could get through, but as I pushed my way along, nearly all of them smiled angelically and said hello. Two of these children live in the same block of flats as I, and we had a little conversation and name exchange, which caused endless giggles.

I made many observations of day-to-day life. The first thing that struck me was that the Egyptians are a race of small build. A tall Egyptian is unusual. I am five feet, five inches, and many are the same height as me. It was also extremely common to see men walking together hand in hand. I don't believe this had anything to do with sexual orientation. They are an excitable people; I would frequently see small groups with someone shouting and wildly gesticulating. It didn't mean there was about to be a fight; they were probably just exchanging views.

I kept passing the same man on the stairs of the flats. The first time I saw him, he was cleaning the stairs. This entailed throwing several buckets of water down them and then sweeping frantically. He was wearing a *galibaya* and had it in his teeth. When he caught site of me, he expressed surprise, stopped sweeping, and saluted! Whenever I saw him, he repeated this salute, which amused me no end. One Friday as I walked downstairs, chairs and rugs and much of the contents of her flat were strung across the landing of the neighbourly lady I had previously encountered. Friday might be the Egyptian equivalent to Sunday, but clearly it was not a day of rest for this family! On my return, I encountered the same man beating the living daylights out of one of the upholstered chairs, using a towel! He stopped, smiled, and of course, saluted!

My opposite neighbour on the landing was an older lady who did not seem to have been in residence until lately. I understand that she has grown up children who live overseas and whom she visits. Whilst sitting on the main balcony one morning, I observed her also on hers. She was standing with something in her hand. I discreetly watched and found that she was holding a thin rope attached to a basket, which was dangling over the balcony on to the street below. She very slowly hauled it up, but I had not seen anybody at the bottom, so I didn't know what she was doing. I had seen other people round Luxor doing this same thing, and I suppose with the absence of lifts in these buildings, it could save an awful lot of going to and fro up and down the stairs.

I could judge the time I awoke each morning by the noise, or lack of it, from outside. Having spent a very disturbed night with the cough despite all the medication, I decided it must be about 6:00 a.m. as it was so quiet. I snuggled back down, but after some time realised it was still quiet. Then the penny dropped, of course: it was Friday. No school, no children, very little traffic, no coming and going. I got up and started the day by cleaning. I was beginning to wonder what exactly was in the pills I was taking, as by 9:15 a.m. I could hardly keep my eyes open. I went back to bed and slept for two hours. The call to prayer at 11:15 a.m. woke me. This went on for over two hours, and I think, being Friday, that the proceedings in their entirety were broadcast through loudspeakers so that everyone could hear it. I was surprised that I hadn't noticed it before, but suspect I had always been occupied with something at the time. I think it is something I will miss, despite the insistence of it. It is all part of the culture and part of the endearment.

There were so many schools in Luxor. I could see three from my own flat, and there were many more. I noticed yet another on the weekly supermarket run and remarked on it to my driver. He told me it was because there were so many children in the town, and that they wanted to build even more schools.

We stopped at the same fruit shop as last week and waited for some time. Two men sitting on the kerb started shouting down the road. Apparently the shop owner was having a cup of tea! Five minutes later he appeared, glass of tea in hand (the tea is always served in glasses, never cups). However, to my amazement, this was not his own tea—he had brought it for me! I declined, thinking he was offering me his own, but he insisted that I drink it, as it was for me. So whilst I picked out my fruit and vegetables, I stood in the street, drinking my tea! I bought some kiwi fruit, and they asked me about them.

"Do you eat them?"

"Yes, I eat them."

They had never seen these before. Whilst paying for my goods, I managed to lose the glass of tea amongst the baskets of fruit. I was not to escape it, however; my noble driver found it for me and told me to drink it up before we got back in the car!

Whilst I went into the supermarket, he went to buy me envelopes and paper for my printer. I had taken a sample of each to show him, and he asked me how many of each. I indicated about an inch of paper and one hundred envelopes. When I returned to the car, he showed me his purchases, asking me for 200LE. I was horrified. Twenty British pounds for paper and envelopes? He laughed and laughed; no, it wasn't money, it was quantity. He had bought me two hundred envelopes and half a ream of paper, and the cost was £4! We drove back to the flat, and he chuckled about it all the way back. I told him how pleased I was with the price, because if it had been 200LE then I wouldn't be sending him shopping again! I suspected he would be retelling this story to many people!

The weather was glorious, about sixty-eight degrees morning and night, with hot days sometimes still reaching one hundred degrees in the direct sun and mid–eighties in the shade. There was no humidity and sometimes a little breeze—absolute perfection. Depending on what time I got up, I did not always breakfast on the balcony anymore, as the temperatures did not start to rise until about 9:30–10:00 a.m., and I noticed that the sun was sinking earlier and the balcony was in the shade by 3:30 p.m. in the afternoons, with sunset at about 5:00 p.m. However, the day-to-day life of the average Egyptian remained unchanged with early rising, a sleep in the afternoon, and the hustle and bustle not dying down until about midnight.

Many Egyptians suffer from diabetes. I had always been surprised by this. However, living amongst them, I am no longer surprised. Everything is laden with sugar. They all take sugar in their tea and coffee, sometimes as much as four spoonfuls, and everything you buy is with added sugar. Even the bread is sweet. I bought some cocoa and found to my horror that it, too, had sugar added. It really was difficult to avoid. It also explained why many Egyptians were fairly portly. Having put on a lot of weight myself after my surgery, I was told when I arrived here that I looked very healthy and much more attractive when I was bigger, and that whilst they understood that this was not so acceptable in Europe, in Egypt it was considered most attractive—ah, deep joy!

There are culinary delights, and then there are culinary experiences. Mine were the latter! Having a day when my cough had kept me awake the previous night and every muscle in my body seemed to be rebelling, I decided I might feel better if I made something substantial and nutritious for my supper. The choice was lentil rissoles. The picture looked lovely: perfect little rounds, crisp and appetizing. I began.

My first problem was the lack of scales; just exactly how many were two-hundred-fifty grams of lentils? I picked up a packet of unopened pasta that had the weight on it and weighed it against my half-used packet of lentils. I took a guess. All was going really well. The lentil mixture was doing its thing, and I had potatoes cooking for mashing and spinach in another saucepan. The lentil mixture was supposed to take fifty minutes. Clearly it was never going to take that long. I added a touch more water as it was getting too thick too quickly. After twenty-five minutes, it was obviously ready. I added the breadcrumbs and stirred it all together. Excellent.

Then came my big mistake. The recipe instructed that you empty the mixture onto a plate and let it cool before shaping it into rissoles and dipping it in flour, beaten egg, and finally in breadcrumbs so it would be ready for frying into those perfect little rounds in the picture. Well, by this time the potatoes and spinach were cooked and ready, and I couldn't afford much time for the mixture to cool. Undeterred, I found a pair of disposable gloves, which I thought would save the heat from my hands. How wrong could one be? It was hot—very, very, hot! In fact, it was scalding. Not to be beaten, I shaped my rissoles, which I realised were much too wet with the extra water I had added. I threw them into the flour, fished about to retrieve them, dropped them in the egg, and plunged them into the bowl of breadcrumbs. Another problem then accosted me. I had not turned the gas on under the frying pan. Now, this was an old-fashioned gas cooker, and one had to light it with a click-on electric lighter. I looked at my hands; they were caked in rissole mixture. Not one to be beaten, I removed a glove and lit the gas. Into the frying pan went the first rissole. It looked fine until I had to turn it over, when of course the whole thing disintegrated. I patted it all together and managed to get it out of the pan and onto a plate. The second rissole followed in much the same manner. I still had two to go, but by now the first one, which was for my supper, was ready and getting cold. So was the mashed potato and spinach. I decided to quit while I was ahead.

I covered everything up, turned off the gas, and ate my supper. Surprisingly, it tasted rather nice, but it looked . . . well, words escape me, really. My thoughts again turned to my mother, who was an excellent cook and prided herself on her presentation. My goodness, she would turn in her grave if she saw this offering!

Supper eaten, I had to return to the kitchen to cook the final two rissoles. It looked like some sort of disaster area. However, finding it much easier now the mixture had cooled considerably, I cooked the final two, which would be put in the freezer, with the third in the fridge for tomorrow. Now I had to clear up. I found to my amazement that there was rissole mixture everywhere—I even found some in a drawer! The electric lighter had it all over the handle, despite my cunning plan of removing the glove. The work surface was covered in flour, there were pans and spoons all over the place, and the whole flat smelled of cooking oil!

Once I set to, it didn't take very long to clean up, and I decided to finish my bottle of brandy, as friends were bringing reinforcements that week. I poured the rest of the bottle into my glass and added the end of the bottle of Coke. There wasn't really enough, but I thought that after the fiasco I had just put myself through, a stiff drink was definitely the order of the day. I had a sip; ah yes, that would make my hair curl!

Regrettably, I had to return to the young man in the carpet shop, as he had promised to get me some stuffing to fill my cushion covers. I knew that this was going to be a tough visit after the first encounter.

If I had ever been in any in doubt about his original intentions when he asked to be "close friends," I was left in no doubt on this occasion. He had never asked anyone to be his close friend before, he told me, not even in England, and he was single, and I was single and on my own. Now, I was unaware that I had a sign on my back saying, "single, available, and desperate." I had never told him that I was here on my own, and in fact had told him that there was a man in my life already in the hopes of putting him off—a ploy that clearly had had no effect whatsoever. Realising that I was getting myself into extremely deep water here, I decided on the blunt approach. I told him that I was quite happy to be friends, but not "close friends," and that that was never going to happen. My problem, of course, was fair skin and fair hair. Even in my current state of needing a tint, there was no denying I was fair!

Undaunted, he made me a cup of tea. Not usually a tea drinker, I can usually manage the Egyptian tea—but this was surely the worst cup of tea I had ever tasted in my life. I asked him for the cushion filler, and to my amazement, he produced yet another pillow with great pride! When I had wanted a pillow it was a nightmare trying to find one, and now I had a second one! He told me he was only charging me what he had paid for it himself, and he was not putting any extra on because he liked me so much. Yeah, right; it cost 10 LE more than the first one I had bought, so I knew he was making £1 out of me! I was unprepared to argue under the circumstances. I gulped down my tea, paid him, thanked him profusely, and told him quite clearly that no, he most certainly could *not* have the kiss he was asking for!

Despite the hassle, I had to smile. I was so overweight at the moment, I had no makeup on, and my hair looked a mess; this was certainly good for morale! It was the only way to look on such encounters, of which there were many. It was obvious why so many middle-aged European women get caught by young Egyptian men, but it would never cease to amaze me how many were so gullible that they signed over all their money and possessions to such men and then found themselves without a penny and with a disappearing husband. There were many who lived in relative poverty, having been caught in this way and without any funds to return to their European homes. Mr. F. had frequently told me of such stories and had made me promise that I would sign nothing at all without consulting him first! He had no need to worry. Whilst I enjoyed the flattery, I was well aware that one had to keep one's feet very firmly on the ground.

On returning home, I split open the pillow and filled my cushion covers. They looked a million times better with a proper filling, and the comfort factor was excellent. So my eventful morning had a successful outcome!

I was still watching my Egyptian soap opera, and it was getting more amusing as it continued. I had only been watching for a few weeks, but in that time there had been five funerals, four weddings, two pregnancies and three marriages ended when the new wife had discovered an existing wife and children! One pregnancy had lasted only about four episodes, and the "bump" had grown alarmingly in that time! However, once born, this baby was never seen, and I began to think I had imagined it until there was an odd reference to the nanny! After the weddings, they all went on honeymoon to the same hotel in Sharm, and I could never decide if it was supposed to be the same, or whether it was supposed to be somewhere different for each couple. In fact, the whole thing reminded me of the early days of *Crossroads*, and one episode in particular, when there was an obvious difficulty in opening a door! The subtitles were attributed to the television company. I think they were trying to be colloquial, but I read things like "I gotta go out now, hun," and, "tell your hubby you wanna come shopping with me." And sometimes, even with my limited sixty-one-word Arabic vocabulary, I knew that the translation wasn't quite as portrayed. Occasionally there would be long sentences uttered and either no subtitle at all, or just a single word of translation. Yet with all its comedic attributes, I loved it, and quite looked forward to stopping whatever I was doing at 5:10 p.m. each day! It was also quite a good way of listening to, and learning, some Arabic, especially the day-to-day words. I wondered if it would still be going on when I came back from the conference, and if so, how many more people would have got married or died in that period!

Fridays continued to confuse me. I had to remember that Fridays were Sundays, and then of course I got mixed up as to whether it was actually Friday or Sunday! On this particular Friday, I drew the curtains back in the dining room and saw a man on the museum roof. He didn't appear to be doing anything, just standing there, facing east. I wondered if he had come quietly up there to pray and watched for a while to see, but I never did figure it out.

The police guards had now changed into their winter uniform of black, rather than white. It was amazing how much more formidable they looked in the darker colour. Many of them were beginning to recognise me now, and I even had a "good morning, Margaret" from one of them. I had watched in amusement one evening as two were dispatched with three large barrels of shredded paper and proceeded to burn it in the small skip opposite. It was obviously well compressed, as it took them well over an hour to burn. The whole time, the smell of rather acrid smoke rose into the air and seemed to get into every corner of the flat.

As I walked along beside the Nile one morning, I was horrified to watch four sailors working in pairs. They were cleaning the stern of the cruise boat, balancing only on some pipes, whilst holding on to another run of pipes above them. There was nothing between them and the river, which was a very long way down. No Health and Safety Department here! It never seems so bad if the people in question are obviously comfortable with what they are doing, but these poor sailors were obviously feeling their insecurity, tentatively feeling their way and looking down to the water, and I hastened on, unable to watch.

Temptation overcame me that morning, and I went in to one of my favourite jewelers, just to browse. The shop is owned by a Christian family, and they do not push you to buy. Today one of the owners was in the shop, and we exchanged the usual pleasantries while I was looking. Before I left, he asked if he could give me some advice. He told me to tell people that I had an Egyptian husband and not to say that I owned a flat here. He said the Egyptian people would not understand why I was living on my own and would consider me to be "fair game." At least, I think that was what he was trying to tell me! I decided to check it out with Mr. F. I could see myself getting into all sorts of tangles with a mythical Egyptian husband. The Egyptians are very forthright in their questions, and I could just imagine forgetting what I had called him and all the fictitious details! However, I did know that the Egyptians found it strange that I traveled on my own. The Egyptian mother is a very central figure in the family, very highly revered, looked after, and usually accompanied. They find it extraordinary that my family permit me to go anywhere on my own and always questioned the fact that no family member traveled with me. As one who cherishes her independence, I have always found that a difficult concept—probably as difficult as they find the converse view!

The other thing I found strange was that I could leave things unattended and have no fear that anyone would take them. When shopping by taxi, the driver frequently accompanied me, leaving the car unattended and unlocked, the windows open and my shopping sitting on the back seat. It just wasn't a problem. I noticed it again one day sitting in the foyer of one of the hotels, having a coffee. One of the reps had obviously based himself there for holidaymakers to book tours or discuss problems. He had gone off to do something else, but left his paperwork, briefcase, credit card machine, and various other documents just sitting on the sofa and coffee table. One just wouldn't do that in the UK, and if you saw bags unattended, you would immediately be suspicious. Despite the fact that one gets a lot of hassle on the streets in Luxor, the basic psyche of the people here is one of trust.

Some English friends, also with a flat in Luxor, came round for coffee one morning. Having lived here much longer than myself, I asked for their help in lighting my gas oven. After five weeks, I was still unable to fathom it out and needed to increase my culinary repertoire! We all took to our hands and knees in front of the oven and had various parts of it out and gas taps turned on. Eventually, we found the elusive burner, and I received good instruction as to its use! The graduation on the dial had long since worn away, but I was told that it really didn't make any difference as these ovens were either on high or low, with no subtle difference between the two!

Mr. F. had sent an electrician round to look at my hot water. In the kitchen it was so hot that you could make a cup of tea with it, and in the bathroom it ran cold so quickly that you couldn't finish a shower. A very presentable man appeared in a leather jacket. He spoke no English, but the problems were easy to convey by pantomime. He produced a screwdriver and took the base off from each boiler, made a few adjustments and declared the problem fixed. To say I was doubtful was an understatement, but whilst I noticed no difference in the kitchen, I did at least get to the end of my shower before it ran cold, and I could see that the thermostat had flicked back on, so it was a small improvement. It really only mattered for a couple of months, because when the weather got warmer, I wouldn't need a lot of hot water for the shower. However, I mentioned it to Mr. F. that night, and he said he would send the man round again the next day.

I also asked him about acquiring an imaginary Egyptian husband. He agreed that this was a good idea because if I said this, I would be left alone and not bothered. Then he volunteered himself as the fictitious candidate!

It struck me from time to time what a cash-based society this was. In the UK I rarely carried much cash, relying mainly on cards, as all the usual shopping could be done with them. Here everything was a cash transaction. They would look at you aghast if you offered a card at the supermarket—not that I had ever tried it. Nothing was geared towards it. The hotels accepted credit cards only, not debit cards. I was forever counting up what was in my purse to make sure I had enough to cover all eventualities when I went out. There was nothing more frustrating than seeing something I needed and had been trying to find, and then not having enough cash to make the purchase.

I was still struggling with the letting agents for my flat in the UK and fighting my corner to get the rent money. Far from having a regular payment date, nobody seemed able to tell me when I would receive this money each month. This was making budgeting a nightmare.

I set out for the baker at the same time in the morning as when I had made my first visit to them. There was no bread there, so I asked about it.

"You want bread?"

"Yes."

"Now?"

"Yes."

He looked at me in complete amazement.

"Later."

"What time?"

"One o'clock."

This seemed unlikely, as most places closed at that time of day and didn't open again until late afternoon. However, I wasn't desperate for the bread; I would try another day.

I made my trip to the post box and then went on to find a shop that I had visited with my German friend earlier in the year. I was delighted that I found it and even more pleased that I found some kitchen scales. I also bought an oblong dish for making lasagne—it just hadn't been the same in a round casserole dish!—a Pyrex bowl for mixing, which also had rather a nifty lid, and a candlestick. The latter required quite an inspired bit of mime, but before I gave up, I managed to find some candles and the problem was solved. The total of my purchases was £13.70—a bargain by English standards—but I found myself now thinking in Egyptian money and finding everything expensive.

On my way back I stumbled across a different baker. He had masses of bread, so I made some purchases—three bagels, a huge date slice, and a cross between a Danish pastry and a croissant—all for 40p! Now that was more like it!

I had been awaiting a phone call from some other English friends who were coming to Luxor to help administrate the conference, a gathering of Egyptological experts giving lectures and site visits. The call came whilst I was at the supermarket, and we arranged to meet at their hotel at 6:00 p.m.

We spent the evening going through everything and making sure that we had tied up all the loose ends. They were off the following day to Aswan and the hotel where the group would be staying to check everything there. I was to stay at the Luxor hotel and meet the group on Monday night. There was to be a welcome meeting on Tuesday morning, and then we would all transfer to Aswan in the Convoy.

We had dinner together and spoke to various members of staff at the hotel to check the details, and I returned home about 11:00 p.m. I decided to type some of the details up and also to email the travel agent in the UK, as we thought we may have found a hiccup in the return ticketing.

I had thought that I hadn't properly relaxed in all the time I had been in Luxor, having had such stress with the letting agents and one thing or another. However, when I got up on Sunday morning, the dawning realisation came—that I had in fact totally relaxed. I got up feeling pressurised; I had things to get ready for the conference, some paperwork that was missing that I had to ring my colleagues about, the flat to close down, and my packing to do. I couldn't get through to my colleagues through their mobile phone, and their hotel wasn't answering, either. Eventually, their phone registered the missed calls, and they rang me so we could sort out the missing bits. That was when it hit me: this was the first morning when I couldn't get up and wander about and just take the day as it came; I had commitments, deadlines, and priorities. My life and my mindset had completely slowed down and changed. The whole reason that I had come here was actually taking shape and coming to fruition without my even realising it.

I rushed about until midmorning and then took some time out. I wandered down to the hotel nearby to treat myself to a pedicure. The young girl who did it spoke very little English at all, and her friend, who knew equally little English, sat beside me sewing the most exquisite gold evening dress with hand-sewn sequins and little flowers. I asked if she had made it, and she said yes. My feet, which had taken a pounding recently from the uneven surfaces, the dust, and the mosquito bites, were pampered to excess. She set about the soles with something that resembled a miniature cheese grater and massaged and painted beautifully. When she had finished, she painted a tiny flower in the bottom corner of each big toenail. It had a dark red centre and tiny white dots all round for the petals. In fact, it was so discreet and tiny that with my appalling eyesight, I could barely see it at all!

I left feeling considerably better and went home for lunch and to continue my preparations for the conference.

In the evening I investigated a lecture I'd been told about. These lectures are held every Sunday at 7:00 p.m. in the Mummification Museum, given by different Egyptologists each week for free. I felt a tad apprehensive, not having been before, but as this was exactly the kind of thing I so enjoyed, I set out with purpose. The usual calls for feluccas, taxis, and caleches, with some of the "hellos" sounding decidedly Leslie Phillips!

I arrived at the museum and was pointed in the direction of a corridor I had never noticed before. I ventured down it and found a small lecture theatre with very comfy seats and a big stage and screen. It was nearly full with about 150 people. I sat in a spare seat at the back on the end of the row. I looked around. To my astonishment, I saw somebody I knew from Sussex Egyptology Society (SES)! I leapt up to say hello and found that I knew the lady in the row behind her and the one in the row behind that! Two were from SES, the other a regular delegate to the conferences who would be joining the forthcoming conference. The lady I had first spotted looked me up and down, telling me I looked absolutely fabulous and that this was obviously suiting me! I felt like a million dollars and it confirmed my realisation of the morning, that yes, I had relaxed and that this small sojourn was actually hitting its mark.

An Italian Egyptologist gave the lecture, in which he gave details of the site he was working on and the various finds they were making there. He spoke perfect English, but it was very, very heavily accented, making it harder to concentrate. As I cast a sneaky look around in case there was anybody else there I knew, I noticed that the lady sitting beside me had nodded off, and she was not alone! It lasted a little under an hour, and he took questions at the end. It was an interesting lecture, and I would try to attend as many as possible on future Sunday nights.

The day of the conference dawned. It was a surreal feeling and one that I had not expected. I really did not want to leave. I was so very happy in my home that I had the same feeling I experienced when closing it up to return to the UK after a holiday. I went round the flat tucking things away, as I knew ten days worth of dust would accumulate; it was better to put things into cupboards as much as possible. I left my bed made, but covered the whole thing with a big king-size sheet. At least I wouldn't have to struggle with making the bed up when I got back late and tired, as I did when I first arrived from the UK.

For the first time it crossed my mind that it was going to be exceptionally difficult when I reached the end of my seven months and returned to pick up my old life in England. After only a few weeks, I was already screaming inside that I didn't want to leave; but of course, I had the best part of six months left, and by that time I might be only too pleased to return! Time would tell.

I popped down to the hotel to have my hair done again so that I looked presentable at least at the beginning of the conference. The hairdresser was delighted to see me back. As he spoke no English, we managed to establish via one of the young assistants that he remembered how he had done my hair before. He asked (via his assistant again) if I had been pleased with the haircut. I said I had been very pleased, omitting details about the stray long bits at the back, which I had tentatively taken scissors to myself! One of my sons-in-law being a hairdresser, I was sure would have been highly amused! However, with the help of "Lacca–very strong," he again managed a very acceptable hairdo, and I left with the same helmet effect. Last time it hadn't moved till about Thursday, and this was clearly going to be the same!

I now had butterflies in my tummy for the impending success, or lack of it, of the conference. I set about the last of the preparations, ready for the taxi to collect me at 2:30 p.m. and take me down to the hotel.

I settled into my hotel room, touched base with a few people, and then treated myself to dinner in the Italian restaurant. The lecturers and delegates arrived at about 11:00 p.m. The rooms were allocated, and I spent some time with "the boss" going through a few things, then joined some friends from Sussex for a drink by the pool.

Next morning we had a welcome meeting, then drove down to Aswan in the convoy after lunch. We settled into our hotel, which would be our base for the next few days.

The conference went well, with trips out to various sites in the mornings and lectures in the afternoons, all peppered with a lot of good food–including a magical dinner on Philae Island one night. The cruise on Lake Nasser followed, and then we went home. We had an early morning wake up call at 3:00 a.m. and left at 3:45 a.m. for the airport at Abu Simbel. The flight to Aswan was about half an hour; then we collected our luggage and the group flew on to Cairo to connect with the Heathrow flight, whilst a fellow delegate and myself got a twenty-minute flight to Luxor. She was returning to the Sheraton for the weekend, where we arranged to meet up, and I was going home!

My little man was sitting waiting for me, ready to carry my case upstairs. He stopped after two flights to shake my hand and say, "Welcome, Madame"—I am sure the only English he knew. I walked into the flat. The overall feeling was calm. It still smelled nice from the various incense I always had burning, and it all looked clean and tidy. Oh, yes, it was so good to be back!

The feeling did not last more than a few minutes; as I walked into the bathroom, the toilet had obviously been used and was filthy. I rang Mr. F. to ask if someone had been in. He told me that there had been a complaint about my water pump—I never really did understand exactly what the problem was—and that they had decided to take the pump fuse out to stop it. They hadn't turned off the electricity, so my freezer had been on all the time. This was a relief. I turned the relative fuse back on and set about cleaning the bathroom. It didn't take long, and with the help of lots of Dettol and Milton Wipes, I was soon happy with its condition.

I unpacked half my things and checked my email. There was one from the letting agent, still unable to tell me when I would regularly receive my rental payments. She suggested that I leave sufficient funds in my bank to cover this situation—what cheek! I was furious, but decided to address it when I was less tired. I had some lunch and straightened out a few more odds and ends; then the early start caught up with me, and I slept soundly for an hour. This turned out to be a terrible mistake, as when I finally decided to go to bed properly at the end of the day, I tossed and turned through the night.

Rising from my siesta, I turned to the last of the unpacking. By now the light was going, so I turned on the bedroom light. Nothing. I tried the dressing table light. Nothing. The bedside light. Nothing. I plugged in a bedside light from the spare room in several different sockets. Nothing. Ah! I thought it had all been going too well. It was obviously a fuse, and I wondered if another one had been taken out with the water pump by mistake. I checked them all, but they were fine. One had a mark on it, so I tried it in the down position just in case there was something different about it, but it made no difference. Mr. F. would start wishing I was still away in Aswan!

I remembered a conversation I had had with someone at the conference. I had been upset, as someone had inferred that I had made a silly decision in coming to Luxor and it hit the mark deep in my psyche somewhere—the insecurity of not wanting to appear foolish. We had discussed the various plumbing difficulties and the fact that things constantly went wrong, although they were always fixed quickly. The person I was talking to found this unacceptable, but I had quickly become accustomed to it. As irritation began to prick with the current electrical problem, remembering the discussion calmed me down. After all, it was only an irritation; it wasn't life threatening, and I had done everything I needed to in that room; I had only to sleep in it, for which I needed it to be dark!

However, I supposed it could be a fire risk if a fuse had blown, so I picked up the phone to Mr. F. I told him the problem, and he said he would look into it right away. He called me back within minutes and said that his son and the electrician would be with me in half an hour. And indeed they were. At precisely 6:30, there was a ring on the doorbell. The same man in the leather jacket was on the doorstep with Mr. F.'s son. We all shook hands, and I showed him the problem. He looked at the fuse box, took off his jacket, and got out his screwdriver, pliers, and fuse wire. He rewired the fuse—the same one that I had noticed had been marked—and within ten minutes, everything was restored. Half an hour later Mr. F. rang to check that it was fixed. This surely was better than anything you could achieve in the UK.

The next morning I walked down to check my post box. The first part of the road had been covered in tarmac—what an improvement! However, instead of ploughing through sand and rubble, I now had to wade through wet tar! I had been told they were doing it all at the same time and working twenty-four hours a day because the president was making a visit. They were trying to get as much finished as possible before his arrival.

On the way back, I bought some fruit. The price was ridiculous, so I said so, and we argued a bit. I told him I was not a tourist, and I wasn't prepared to pay those sort of prices, and he reduced it immediately. I stopped and bought more bread, then called in at the small supermarket for yoghurt and frozen fish. The supermarket was in chaos, as they were receiving a delivery. Boxes and containers spilled out all over the pavement. I fought my way in, picked up what I wanted, and went through the usual fiasco at the till.

How I had missed all this in the cocoon of the hotels and cruise boat, and how much more at ease I felt returning to it again. Yes, it was definitely good to be home.

December/January

A day spent cleaning in preparation for my first visitor exacerbated my tennis elbow. It had been such a relief when it had eased, but housework here was so heavy duty, and I think the Hoovering and mopping upset it. Upright Hoovers didn't seem to exist, only the type you pull along behind, which necessitate two hands on the pipe in a sweeping motion. On top of that, most of the floors were tiled and needed washing regularly, involving a similar range of movement. On reflection, life here reminded me a great deal of my early childhood, when my mother didn't work outside the home and spent all day, every day, cooking and cleaning. She cleaned every morning, did the washing on Monday, the ironing on Tuesday, and cooked every afternoon. Washing was always hung in the garden, and floors invariably scrubbed on hands and knees. There were no microwaves or convenience foods, and the shopping was done at the local shops.

Life here followed the same pattern. I admit to not cleaning every day, but I did clean several times a week. I cooked from scratch, as convenience foods were just not available in the same way. Frozen food was available in its raw form, not as pre-packaged meals. I actually enjoyed the cooking, as I had time to do it and time to give a little thought to what I was going to prepare. Shopping was also much as I remembered it in my childhood.

I had had an interesting exchange one morning in my small local supermarket. I went in for milk and cheese, but bought some frozen vegetables and a couple of cans of lemonade whilst I was there. I could see the hard cheese that I needed, but nobody was about. I asked the friendly chap at the checkout, with whom I had chatted before, for help. He sent a man over to the cheese fridge. I pointed to the cheese I wanted, but I could only buy it in its entirety. It was a huge block such as they cut smaller pieces from to sell in Tesco. As an alternative, he produced a smaller box of processed cheese. It would have to do. I went back to the checkout. Whilst packing my shopping, he asked if I lived here. Ah, I could see what was coming, so best to pre-empt it.

"Yes, I live here; I have an Egyptian husband." That should do the trick.

Something complimentary followed, but I couldn't catch all of it, so I decided just to smile sweetly back and not ask! He told me the price, and I paid. He produced the correct change. This was a first in this shop; no matches or sweets to make up the difference. But before handing it to me, he took out the calculator and re-checked the price. There is a till, but it doesn't work, and the man at the till always used to be a calculator, with the money just being stuffed in a drawer. I was given the change, and he told me it was a special Egyptian price because I was an Egyptian. I knew there was a difference in tourist price and local price for lots of things, but whether it applied to food, I was unsure. However, at just under £3 for two bags of shopping, I really wasn't going to argue, so I thanked him profusely and set off for home!

This was the first day that I had seen bare-footed children in the street, and I wondered how on earth they managed it. I found it difficult enough in shoes walking over the dust and rubble that abounded; I just couldn't imagine what it would feel like without. Thinking about it as I walked on down the road, I was doubly amazed to pass a workman digging a big hole, again with nothing on his feet. I carried on home, thinking how privileged we really are in the West and resolving to try not to grumble about life quite so much in the future.

A new day dawned, and I woke up finding I was scratching my hand. I had been bitten on three fingers and all up one arm. I dressed and went to the mirror to brush my hair. Oh no! I had also been bitten all over my face and neck, giving me the appearance of Spotty Muldoon on a good day! I remembered hearing something buzzing during the night. Goodness knows how they got in; I thought it was too cold for mosquitoes now. My guess was that flies had bitten me, and whilst there are not many, it only takes one!

A friend and delegate from the conference had introduced me to a local Egyptian friend who was going to a hotel furniture sale. I was after two comfortable chairs for my balcony to replace the less comfortable plastic variety. I spoke to the Egyptian on the phone, and he said he would find two nice ones for me. Later that day, he rang to say that his cousin would bring them to the flat for me. Two wonderful bamboo chairs appeared, but without cushions. I made another phone call to arrange to get some cushions made.

Next day, a car arrived to collect me, and we went to a tiny shop in Luxor. We went down an alley and round the back into a derelict building that would have been condemned in Europe. Inside were vast quantities of foam in various sizes and thicknesses. I chose what I needed and we went back round to the shop. Now came the nice part: choosing the fabric. I decided that whilst I was doing this, I might as well have some cushions made for the chairs for the table on the balcony, and I had stuck four pieces of paper together and drawn round them to make a template. The Egyptians thought this was hilarious; I had thought it was rather good! The little old man at the sewing machine asked if I was giving him a map! I chose the material, and he said he would make them with zips so that they could be washed. The material was like a light canvas, which I was told I must have to withstand the sun. The old man would start to make them the following evening, and I would get them the day after. The price was about £26 for four zipped seat cushions, four very large zipped chair cushions, and one elastic bedroom stool cushion. I was delighted.

We then returned to the restaurant owned by my new Egyptian friend. It had been open six months, and he wanted to show me. It was amazing: spotlessly clean and beautifully furnished and finished. He insisted that I stayed to have something to eat, on him. The food was some of the best I had eaten in Egypt; I would certainly be a regular customer.

From there we went on to meet an Australian lady. She lived in a flat above the restaurant and had just opened a shop. He thought that I would like her and would enjoy looking at the things in her shop. We got on well instantly. She told me she had lived in Luxor for seven years, but the shop had only been open a couple weeks. It was an Aladdin's cave of goodies, crafts, and gifts: nice cotton and towels and everything with a price tag—something you never, ever see in Egypt. Since I passed the end of the road every week on my way to and from the post office, we arranged that I would call in and have a proper look in the shop and have a chat.

I returned home deeply content. Upon waking the next morning, I realised just how happy I was. I was beginning to make friends, find my way about, and feel that I belonged. Despite all the little annoyances that went with life here, I felt happier than I had for a long time.

December 8 was the first day I needed a coat to go out in the evening. Really, it was too hot with a coat, but too cold without it. The middle of the day was still hot, but as soon as the sun started to sink, a new chill filled the air.

A clothes rail had appeared in the museum kitchen courtyard. I watched with amusement as one of the waiters changed into his uniform and very carefully hung his clothes up on the rail. I am sure he would have been horrified if he knew I was watching him, but there were two blocks of flats, all with windows looking this way, so surely he must have realised. I noticed a new prayer mat and a few other changes round the courtyard. The chef put in an appearance, with the air of being totally in charge, holding himself erect and surveying all around him! It was still a source of great entertainment to me.

The following day I wandered up to check my post. I found two Christmas cards addressed to a previous occupier of my box. There was no one to tell, so I left them on the desk. I had only gone a few steps down the road when they were calling me back. I went back and tried to explain, showing my own post with my name and indicating that the name on the other two cards was different. They nodded their understanding, and I wondered what would happen to these two cards.

I stopped at the baker and bought my bread for the week and then called in to the Australian lady's shop. She made me a cup of coffee and we chatted. When I looked at my watch I found I had been with her nearly three hours! There had been so much to talk about! We made arrangements to meet up again a few days later and resume our conversation, and I left for home.

My next task was to cook, and I decided to make a fish pie with some frozen fish I had. I'd make one for me and one for the freezer. All was going well until I picked up the fish, which I had left defrosting that morning. Ah, this was not the white, flaky fish I had anticipated. No matter, it would be fine. All went well in my flurry of cooking and washing up, and at last it was ready. I put my portion on a plate with some vegetables and sat down to eat.

Now, here was a surprise! I really wasn't at all sure what it was that I had just cooked, but I rather suspected it was squid. It was actually very nice, just not what I was expecting. It reminded me of the first time I cooked choux pastry when I was first married. I was following the recipe and trying to achieve what was in the picture, absolutely convinced that I was making meringue!

The day was running away with me; by now it was nearly 4:00 p.m., and I had an invitation to join an American archeologist and his wife on their houseboat for sunset. I had promised to be there by 4:30 p.m., and I had a good ten minute walk. I got myself ready, and as I closed up the kitchen balcony, I spotted two fire engines in the Corniche. Their hoses sprayed into the river, and a big crowd of emotional Egyptians were shouting and gesticulating and running around. My first thought was that the museum must be on fire, but when I glanced down into the kitchen courtyard, everything appeared normal. I walked downstairs and out into the street. The guard on the barrier, who is always there, would not let me through. He spoke no English, so although I tried to find out what was going on, he couldn't tell me and just indicated that I must walk round the block to get back to the Corniche. I did this, looking back to see if I could see anything, but I was none the wiser.

I arrived at the Mummification Museum, through which I had to walk to get to my destination. I then had to clamber over a gangplank with no handrail. I was really wishing I wasn't wearing such a long skirt! I hitched it up and balanced my way across. Then I went over two adjacent boats, one with quite a gap that I just tried not to think about as I crossed it. At last I was there. What a wonderful boat it was; it felt like stepping back in time. We sat with glasses of wine, watching the sunset and talking. Life really couldn't be much sweeter. How very, very lucky I was to have all these wonderful opportunities.

The cold night of December 8 had not been repeated. Two nights later, I had the windows open until I went to bed, and the air felt much warmer again. It was hard to remember that it was nearly Christmas. I had three Christmas cards on display and thought I would put up my candlelights as a token gesture and to welcome my friend arriving the next day.

Another plumbing problem had arisen and been solved. My large boiler that served the kitchen was wasted in that location, as the washing machine and dishwasher were plumbed to cold only, and I only needed hot water for washing up and cleaning. Conversely, the bathroom boiler was much too small, and the water was still running cold by the time I got to the end of my shower. Mr. F. thought this was very funny, and I tried hard to explain that as a woman, it took me longer under the shower. Not only that, but there would be three women in the flat during the next week. He laughed and arranged to send the man round to change them over.

A ring on the doorbell heralded the boiler man's arrival; it was the man in the leather jacket who had been here before! I thought he was an electrician, but it seemed he dabbled in plumbing, too! We shook hands and passed pleasantries, he in Arabic, me in English, and he set to work.

First thing was to drain the boilers. Now, I would have thought the easiest way would be to run all the taps, but I found to my amazement that he had just taken the fixings off the walls—the water was pouring out all over the floor! True, there were drains in all the floors, but not for this quantity of water! I pointed with horror when I saw it lapping a rather nice rug in the hallway, and he asked for a mop. I took up the rug and gave him the mop, with which he just swept the flood towards the drain. Next was a little pile of sandy looking material, which I assumed was in the bottom of the boilers. No wonder the tap filters got blocked up. This was then trodden through various parts of the flat. How I wished I hadn't bothered to wash the floors that day! However, it only took about forty minutes, and the plumber's job was complete. Off he went, and off I set with mop and bucket and Dettol for the toilet, which seemed to have become covered in dirty water.

I was delighted with the result, managing to shower and wash my hair with hot water continuously. However, just as I was about to go out that evening, I noticed water leaking from one of the fixing points and a steady rivulet making its way across the bathroom floor to the drain. I rang Mr. F. I was sure it only needed tightening, but I didn't have the tools to do it. Mr. F. arranged for the same man to come back at 9:00 p.m. Nine o'clock came and went, and at 10:00 I decided to go to bed. I was pleased that I had, as he turned up at 11:00 the next morning! Nevertheless, a quick turn with the giant pliers and all was fixed amidst much shaking of hands and prolific thanks.

The building opposite had not grown noticeably. Some breeze-block inside walls had gone up on the top floor, but there didn't seem to be much activity at the moment. I kept looking at the brickwork and wondering why it looked different, and then it struck me. None of the bricks were pointed. I compared them with brickwork at the nearby school and found that this was the same. It looked remarkably like the old mud brick houses of Pharaonic times.

I looked at my calendar. It was six weeks since my haircut, and the mirror was telling me it was time for another. I went back to the same place with more than a bit of apprehension. After all, last time they had had a cut to follow; by this time, the basic English cut was gone. I walked in and was recognised and offered a seat. A telephone call was immediately made to summon the hairdresser, who never seems to be there unless called. To my dismay, the man who appeared was not the same one, despite my having asked for him by name. I offered up a little prayer and had my hair washed.

It was a totally different experience. I felt this man considered himself something of an artist. He went to enormous trouble to cut my hair—none of the fast and furious stuff of before! There was much clicking of the scissors, but when he got round to a part I could see, I realised that although he was clicking a lot, he wasn't actually cutting very much! The back and sides done, he approached the front with a razor. Now this was worrying; this was the bit I could see and would have to look at for the next six weeks! He turned my head away from the mirror to face him, and when I eventually turned back, I was absolutely horrified to see my fringe cut with a huge gap in it, reminding me of a haircut I gave my children when they were small, the one and only time I every attempted it! However, he then ran his fingers all through it and I could see that the basic shape was good. He laughed and said that it was finished, so I said if it was finished he wasn't getting any money, and we laughed together. The finished result wasn't too bad, although I doubted its staying power. I didn't have the concrete-helmet effect this time and was able to go home and add a few finishing touches, which satisfied my vanity.

A few hours later I was sitting in the taxi at the airport, awaiting a text from my friend, Pam, to say she was in the baggage hall. The text came, and I wandered up to the arrivals door. I was very entertained by the reps I was standing with, especially when they started to call out, "Thomas Cook," "Kuoni," and other names. I really felt I should join in with "Davies Tours"! I waited and waited. All the reps started to leave, their holidaymakers ticked off their various lists and their buses full. I realised I was standing alone, and my friend nowhere to be seen. I eventually got another text asking, "Where are you?" to which I replied, "Right outside the door." Then I heard my name, and there she was coming back from the car park. She had managed to walk straight past me, and because she was in the middle of a large group of people, I hadn't seen her. No matter; after many greetings and felicitations, we were soon back in the taxi speeding towards home.

We unpacked the little Christmas tree that I had left in a bag for her to bring across for me when she came to visit, plugged it in, and put a few presents around it, accompanied by my one and only Christmas CD. A glass of Pimms completed the scene, and we laid the table with a Christmas tablecloth and serviettes and two red candles.

I allowed a day for Pam to recover from traveling, and then we were off on the train to Minya with our young Egyptian companion, who had booked and arranged it all for us. I think we laughed continuously from the moment we set off. It had crossed my mind that being with two giggly, middle-aged women was going to be a bit much for our companion, but he joined in with good spirit and often made us laugh all the more. At the end of the weekend he said how much he had enjoyed our company, so perhaps we hadn't been that difficult!

We arrived at the station in Minya, where a local Egyptian met us and whisked us off to the hotel. We found our room fairly basic, but that had been my fault. I was not keen to see how much money we could spend, so I had chosen a three-star hotel rather than a four-star one. It somehow added to the hilarity. The bathroom was tiny, and the door was a plastic concertina type with a broken handle, so we couldn't really close it properly—lucky then that we were such good friends! The window was huge and gave a wonderful panoramic view over the Nile, but it rattled all night! However, we spent so little time at the hotel that it really didn't matter.

On our first day, we set off for a long drive in a minibus with our new guide. We crossed the river on a ferry, which was an experience in itself. This part of Egypt does not have many tourists, and we were nearly always the only Europeans wherever we went, which caused much staring and great interest. We drove through little villages with children waving and various livestock running around and eventually got to Amarna. We covered the tombs and the palace and took lots of photos, despite a great wind that was blowing sand everywhere—not good for two contact-lens wearers!

When we got back to the hotel, we were given some suggestions of places to eat. We decided we would like to eat on a *dahabeya*. We had to choose what we would like to eat before we boarded. On the way, we stopped at a toy shop, as I had to buy a birthday present for a small child in Luxor. We laughed as we played with the various toys, especially a small hand puppet with a squeak inside and a tongue that flew out, which was what I eventually bought. We went on to the boat, where we sat down at a table and nearly got blown away. The wind was quite severe; we couldn't even keep the tablecloth on the table! After more laughter, we decided to go downstairs to the only cabin. Here there was a large square table, rather like a boardroom table, just for the three of us. We had a hilarious meal, helped by a secret bottle of white wine, which we had to hide as the boat was not licensed!

Next morning, poor Pam was hit by a bad tummy, so we left a little later than planned in order to give her tum time to settle. Then we took a long drive to Tuna el-Gebel, which was quite magical. We saw lots of desert, a boundary stela, and some tombs. Then we were off again back to Beni Hassan. Here we met much Egyptian negotiation, as the governor was visiting that day and there seemed to be a problem. I was aware of money changing hands, and then we went off up the many, many steps to the top of the mountain and into the tombs. By now we were running out of time to catch the train, so we quickly dashed back to the hotel, took a wash and collected our luggage, then ran back to the station. We need not have worried. Although the trains run amazingly to time when you catch them from their starting destination, at halfway along the route, this train arrived nearly an hour late.

We settled into our seats for the next seven hours. The refreshments man came along every twenty minutes, calling "tea," and, "coffee" in Arabic, but every time he got to us, he said it very quietly in English! We had far more cuppas than we would normally have had, purely because he was making such an effort!

We got back to Luxor shortly after 11:00 p.m., and our Egyptian friend found us a taxi. I asked the driver if he would carry our bag up, and he said no, so I asked him for change for the fare. He said he didn't have any. Ah, negotiation time! I explained that if he carried the bag up for us, he could keep the change, and that achieved the desired result!

We spent the next couple of days reliving our wonderful weekend and laughing again at the many things that had tickled our funny bones along the way.

Monday saw the arrival of my old school friend CJ, who was coming to spend Christmas and New Year. I went off again to the airport, but this time I spotted my visitor with no problem. We got back to the flat, and Pam had turned on the Christmas lights and made it all look cosy. We made introductions and had Pimms to celebrate, followed by a glass of pink champagne that CJ had brought with her. We had more presents under the little tree and a box of chocolates—such a special treat!

The next morning, we walked into Luxor and went to visit the Australian lady's shop. We were warmly greeted and spent a very amusing half hour while my two visitors tried various things on amidst instructions and suggestions for colour and method of wearing. A coffee at one of the hotels followed, and on the way home we booked a table for dinner at the Old Winter Palace for Pam's last night and CJ's first.

We invited our Egyptian friend from the "Minya Adventure" to join us for coffee after dinner. It was a lovely evening enjoyed by all, and my two visitors insisted that it was their treat.

Wednesday dawned, with Pam going home that afternoon. We decided on a quick trip to the Valley of the Kings, where we saw three tombs. Pam and CJ did a walk with one of the local Egyptians to the top of a ridge to take photos. I decided against it, as I was still struggling with my cough. I sat and waited for them to come back. Of course, a local Egyptian immediately accosted me. I ended up spinning the usual line of the Egyptian husband. Unfortunately, he kept asking questions about this husband: where did we meet? What was his name?. In desperation, I texted my AWOL friends to hurry them back!

We went back to the flat for lunch, packing, and a short nap for Pam before she was off in the taxi to the airport. For me, it was an emotional farewell. We had had such fun, and it was hard to see her go. I went back upstairs, and despite the earliness of the hour, I was quite my usual self after a stiff brandy and Coke!

We had a quiet couple of days after that, the first with lunch out at a Nile-side café, and the second in a joint effort on the housework. We were ready for the next day when we would shop and do various chores in preparation for Christmas Day.

Christmas food shopping was in complete contrast to the mania of the same in the UK. The supermarket had a few more people in it than usual, but it wasn't really that noticeable. Our shopping bill was about £30. We went off to the fruit and veg man, where we spent about £5—quite an extravagance! We bought strawberries and fresh mushrooms, which I had never seen before or since in Luxor. He also had chestnuts, which some other English ladies were buying. We took a trip the next day to the duty-free shop, where we managed to buy Egyptian "champagne" called Aida! It proved to be quite drinkable, which was a pleasant surprise!

Christmas Day dawned and was quite different from any other I had experienced. First of all, it was an ordinary working day. The children were still at school, the shops were all open, and everyone was working as usual. We started our day with a Buck's Fizz on the balcony, where we opened a few presents. I made many phone calls and texts to my darling daughters and their youngsters and several friends. All my grandchildren spoke to me, even the one-year-old, who told me that Father Christmas said, "Oh, oh, oh!" My eldest granddaughter spoke only in whispers, making it difficult to understand anything she said to me, but my grandson gave me a robust rendition of "Jingle Bells" with great emphasis on the "one horse open sleigh-ay!!" Christmas lunch was a make-it-up-as-you-go-along type of tinned salmon in a mushroom sauce with filo pastry, which tasted surprisingly good, followed by Christmas pud and brandy sauce that CJ had brought with her. We returned to the balcony for coffee and more presents. It was a completely stress-free day, which would be long-remembered. The Coptic Christmas is January 7, so Christmas would be an extended one this year.

The New Year, however, is celebrated in style in Egypt. CJ and I went out to eat. We had an excellent dinner, with a bottle of Obelisk rose wine and a free dessert buffet. It became quickly apparent that most people had dined early; in fact, we were the last to leave at 10:30 p.m., most people going on to celebrate elsewhere. We returned home by midnight. It was an emotional time for me, as always; it is a time of year I do not enjoy at all, bringing to mind various unhappy events of previous new years and the nostalgia of all the looking back over the past twelve months. However, just as I was getting depressed, I opened the dining room window and heard a countdown. Then all the cruise boats sounded their sirens and hooters, rising to an enormous cacophony; it lifted my mood immediately. No sooner had the noise started to subside than my phone rang with friends from England, realising that it was midnight for me and ringing to wish me a happy New Year. I was thrilled, and it quite made the evening for me.

So, a new year was dawning, and who knew what would be in store?

New Year's Day brought CJ's return to the UK. We spent a leisurely morning and walked down to the Nile-side café to have lunch. We chose a seafood spaghetti, which was huge and cost £1.50! We went home to close up the suitcase, and then the taxi arrived promptly at 2:00 p.m. to whisk my friend away.

It seemed strange after three weeks of visitors and fun, to be back on my own again. I went down to the Mercure that afternoon and treated myself to a pedicure to take my mind off it. It was an enjoyable experience with a different girl this time. She put a new design on my big toes, all very pretty, but sadly they did not match each other, which rather spoilt the effect!

Next day I called in to the Australian lady to say happy New Year. I met another English lady there who lives in Karnak; I had noticed her at the cheese counter in the supermarket before Christmas. We chatted for a while, and then I returned home via my post box where I collected two New Year's cards from friends.

Winter appeared to have been and gone with the few cold days between Christmas and New Year's Day. I had found it necessary to buy a small, three-bar electric fire, but had only put it on for three evenings. On the last evening, I frightened myself when, on turning it off, I realised that the floor was so hot that I could not touch it! It had been turned off for an hour before I went to bed, but I could still only just touch it for the heat—thank goodness the floors are solid and not floorboards! I had been contemplating buying a blanket to go over the duvet, but by the time the shops were open after the Egyptian holiday, the weather had warmed.

The Egyptian Hajj Feast coincided with the New Year and ran on either side of it. The Hajj is the pilgrimage to Mecca and a cause of enormous celebration once it is finished. Similar to the feast at the end of Ramadan, the shops all closed, and the whole town quietened whilst Egyptian families all got together and celebrated. It was nearly a week before the post office re-opened and I could get to my mail.

By January 4, the workmen had returned to the building opposite. At the end of the day, I watched as two of the men washed under a standpipe, one washing his hair with copious quantities of soap. Considering how cold the water must have been, I was amazed that he washed his legs and feet and wandered off with no towel in sight. The second chap had a towel with him—good thinking! Beside the standpipe was a tall pottery jar. Another man in a galabeya seemed to be in charge of this. It was filled every morning from the standpipe and had a ladle in it. It appeared that anyone could drink from here, and the guards from the police office often did so. I had even seen passers-by lift the wood off the top and take a ladle of water to drink.

The workmen had also returned to the flat below me. When I looked in the open door, I could see that all the banging was because they were hammering off the tiles on the walls from the kitchen, cloakroom, and bathroom. One morning, there was a terrible crash, and my ornamental wooden mask fell off the wall and split in two. I picked up the pieces and went downstairs. Much pantomime followed. They explained that it would stick with glue, so I suggested they might like to mend it. It got me nowhere, except that I felt better for expressing my anger! Some days later, my taxi driver took me to a furniture workshop, and whilst we waited in the taxi, a lovely man took my mask and stuck it back together for me. He asked for £1, so I gave him £1.50, as I was so delighted with the result. The mask had come from my family home as a child, and my parents had collected them, so it was a sentimental piece. Next time I heard the hammers going downstairs, I took it swiftly off the wall!

After all the celebrations of Christmas and New Year, I realised with horror that my Visa was about to run out. Terrified I would be sent home early, I rang Mr. F. to check what I must do. By now the passport office was closed for the day, so I rang for a taxi to collect me at 9:30 a.m. the following morning. He arrived promptly, and I asked him if we could go via somewhere that I could photocopy my passport and current visa, as I remembered from a previous time that this would be necessary. We stopped along the way, and he took my passport and had the necessary copies done. When I asked him how much it cost, he just said, "It is nothing, only small money."

I couldn't imagine any taxi driver in London not only stopping at the kerbside to make some photocopies, but also paying for it! We went on to the passport office, and I paid my fare plus a large tip, which would cover the cost of the photocopies.

I entered the office in fear and trepidation. Last time I had done this with Mr. F. as part of my flat purchase, it had taken all morning—hours of hanging around and waiting. A policeman greeted me at the door and asked what I needed, then pointed to a counter at the end. I realised at once the benefit of going this early, as I was one of the only people there. I found a nice lady, who gave me a form to complete. I filled it in quickly and handed it back to her with my photocopies and a small photo. She told me that to renew the visa for six months would be 61.25 LE. I gave her 62 LE, not expecting any change. She told me to come back in one hour. It was disarming to leave without my passport, but I put on a brave face and crossed the road to the hotel opposite, where I had coffee and passed the hour at leisure.

Thinking that it would probably be an "Egyptian hour," I didn't hurry back, but returned after an hour and ten minutes. I went to the same lady. Five minutes more, she told me. I sat down opposite her counter, amidst many others, mostly Egyptians. I had come prepared and got my magazine out of my bag and settled in for a wait: an Egyptian five minutes could be up to an hour. I was quite engrossed in the article I was reading when I realised the man next to me was trying to attract my attention. I looked up, and he pointed at the counter. The lady was standing there, waving my passport! Delighted, I went to collect it. She told me that I must get 75 piastres from the cashier—my change. Wow, this was a first! She walked down her side of the counter to make sure I went to collect it. I think the cashier was as surprised as me; after all, we were only looking at about 7p, and this sort of change is just never given in Egypt! However, despite his surprise, he found 75 piastres for me, and I set off for home.

Although it was a long walk back, I didn't have to rush, and it was cool enough to be pleasant. I noticed with amusement that, whilst I was wearing long trousers, a long-sleeved sweatshirt, a sleeveless fleece, and a denim jacket with trainers and socks, most of the tourists I passed were in cropped trousers, open-toed sandals, and T-shirts. Perhaps I was becoming more Egyptian: I didn't think it was that hot! As I walked along, one of the little mini-buses stopped to let someone off. I heard an extraordinary noise and wondered what it was. The sudden realisation dawned that it was the man who had just got off the bus. He was holding two live chickens upside down by their feet, and they were complaining!

I got back home, delighted with the progress of my morning, only to find that the hammering had begun again downstairs. My wooden mask lay on the floor in three pieces. Disappointed, I decided that this mask was not meant to be on the wall here. I gathered up the pieces to put in a drawer. I couldn't quite bring myself to throw them away. Maybe someday in the future I'd piece them together once again, but for now I would search out something new to go on the empty hook.

A couple of days later, I went down to see Mr. F. via my Australian friend's shop. She was diligent in her search for something to replace my mask, and eventually we hit upon a small mirror in the shape of an open window. Made in Cairo from decorated brass, it was just the thing, and I was delighted. I discussed with her my difficulty in finding inexpensive serviette rings, and she said she would look in Cairo next week when she was off on a buying spree for the shop.

My walk to her shop had been circuitous! They were laying tarmac in the road right up to her turning. I was walking behind two Muslim ladies who had stopped, I thought, to ask for an alternative route. With confidence, I followed them down into the Souk, only to find they went into a restaurant! So I braved the Souk alone, not having the faintest idea where I was or how to get to my friend's shop. I was pleasantly surprised that I was able to walk through without too much attention, mostly because there were many tourists who were stopping to look as I marched resolutely onwards. However, when I did eventually realise where I was, I had arrived at the main street, some way past where I was intending to go! I walked back down the road, only to meet the new tarmac again, but realised with relief that I could just get to the correct turning by some mountaineering over all the rubble!

When I left the shop to get to Mr. F.'s office, I had a similar problem. My friend directed me through the Souk, and I set off again. I emerged on a road that I had never seen before in my life! I hesitated, and immediately an Egyptian man came up to ask me what I was looking for. I told him the police station, hoping this might put him off, and knowing that it was near Mr. F.'s office. I was only a stone's throw away, and he directed me efficiently, passing me a card for his restaurant as I thanked him and left!

I spent a couple of hours with Mr. F., and we talked about my cooker, which had caused me such consternation. Cooking with the calor gas still worried me, especially since I hadn't turned it off properly over Christmas, and only the smell of gas had alerted me. Evidently I had frightened Mr. F. to death, and he said he would ask his son to see whether he could find an electric cooker for me. I suspected this would be quite a task, as I had never seen an electric cooker in Luxor, and I had been keeping an eye out. However, I fervently hoped he was successful in his quest. Apart from my anxiety with the gas, the cooker was old, and despite all my cleaning, it never really felt or looked clean.

I had a similar problem with the fridge, which always looked grubby despite all my efforts. It was also making an awful noise, its motor on most of the time in its endeavour to keep everything cold. Next morning I decided to do a little research of my own on the fridge front. I went to two nearby shops and found exactly what I was looking for in both, but the prices were much more expensive than I had anticipated. I felt the cooker situation was more pressing, so the fridge would have to wait. I would mention it to Mr. F. though, because the prices become much cheaper if it is an Egyptian who is asking!

In the afternoon I went to visit my neighbour who lives opposite. I had had pressing invitations from her to call in. After checking with an Egyptian friend about protocol, I had rung the day before and asked if I could call in the next afternoon. I arrived at 3:00 p.m. as we had arranged. She was delighted to see me, and we sat on her balcony, where she produced a dish of boiled sweets. I took one and thanked her, then had great difficulty talking to her with the sweet in my mouth, which seemed to last forever! She told me that she was much closer to the river than me. We took a little tour of her flat, with her opening windows for me to see the view. I was amazed. She only lived across the landing form me, but the difference in the view was amazing. I felt I could reach out and touch the Nile.

We went back to the balcony after I had admired her wedding photographs, and she made coffee and brought biscuits, insistent that I should eat. Her English was much better than I had anticipated from speaking with her briefly outside our doors. She was interesting to talk to; she told me about local people and the other people who lived in the building. I looked at photographs of her children, from now and from when they were small. She brought fruit for me to eat, and we discussed the differences in sleeping and eating times between Egyptians and English and how it changed again as the heat of summer arrived. I spent an hour and a half with her and thoroughly enjoyed it. As I left, she repeated her invitation for me to come anytime. She said that if I needed any help at all, she would always be very happy to assist.

The hammering from downstairs was reaching a crescendo. I noticed that all the windows had been taken out, and now they were taking up the floors. There really would be nothing at all left except the shell. Knowing the lack of any safety regulations here, I began to wonder whether my fourth floor flat would soon become a third- or even second-floor apartment. I had learned from my neighbour that the flat under construction belonged to a company and that various employees used it. I could only assume that the company had decided to upgrade. Perhaps this had had something to do with the fact that the stairwell was plunged into darkness one evening, as clearly the plumbing and electrics were being replaced, too!

I had still been experiencing problems with my water. The new pump, which did a fantastic job, would not switch off. It was working continuously, and I had to turn it off at the fuse box when I did not need water for anything. Eventually, a team of three arrived. They seemed to completely rebuild both toilets, and after nearly four hours, they pronounced the fault solved. We checked everything together, and I was delighted. On enquiry as to the cost, I was told it was £16 for the three of them! All went well for twenty-four hours, and then I realised that the water pressure was down; the washing machine struggled to fill, and when I went to wash my hair, only a trickle came out of the shower. A visit to Mr. F. the next day promised the workmen's return visit to try to solve the problem yet again.

Next to solve was the satellite for the TV. I had been in the middle of watching something when it just switched itself off, and I couldn't get it back on. The man arrived within half an hour of my calling him and set to work with great diligence. I explained that I didn't understand any of it (as my daughters would confirm!). He went to great lengths to explain, and he moved all the English-speaking channels to the top of the list so I would not have to search for them. He left an hour later, leaving me with a choice of 935 channels!

The next excitement was the president's visit. Nobody seemed to know exactly which day he was coming, which

I was told was for security reasons. The streets of Luxor were swept to within an inch of their lives on Saturday, and banners and posters appeared everywhere along the route which he would take. On Sunday, I noticed that all the cars in Museum Street were moved into an adjacent empty piece of land, and policemen lined both sides of the road, facing down the side streets. They stood quite still for about twenty minutes and then started to shuffle and talk to each other, which amused me greatly when I thought about the UK military who line routes for the Queen, unmoving and silent for hours. After a couple of hours, I was aware of a cavalcade of vehicles rushing down the road, and half an hour later, the soldiers dispersed. The Corniche, which had been emptied of all people—tourists and locals alike—was beginning to look more busy, and I could only assume that the Great Man had passed by!

The following day saw the return of my plumbers for the water pump. I had just left the flat and was walking down the road when I received the call, so I turned around and went back. Two of them arrived this time and seemed to know exactly the problem. After about half an hour, we all walked round the kitchen and bathroom, turning on taps to check. It seemed that I must run the tap for a while first to activate the pump, and then I had good water pressure. I thanked them profusely before they left.

Pleased with the result, I reported in to Mr. F. by phone and then left on my original shopping expedition. As I reached the Corniche, I realised that again the road was lined with soldiers. In fact, every road was shielded this way as I walked the couple of miles to where I needed to go. I felt sorry for those men standing on the town side, as many were just facing brick walls; on the other side of the road, the soldiers at least had the river and passers-by to look at. I wasn't sure where I was allowed to walk, so I pressed on regardless.

I walked to the kitchen shop and bought some small glasses, a guest towel, a cheese slicer, a corkscrew, and four cereal bowls. The total bill was just over £9. I retraced my steps home. However, this time as I came up to the Old Winter Palace, I realised that the president must be inside. Many cars, all very official looking, were parked outside, and the hotel had a new awning out. There were security guards everywhere. The strange thing was that I was allowed to walk across the hotel unchallenged, but when I went to cross the road, one of the soldiers stepped into my path and firmly told me "no." I checked with him about walking up on this same side, and that appeared to be fine. How strange. I got to the crossroads by the temple, where again there were dozens of security police. I looked farther up the road and could see no pedestrians at all and several guards in the temple complex itself, the temple clearly closed to visitors. By now feeling a little weary and not bothering to ask, I cut down to the back of the town and walked back that way.

As I passed the post office on this route, I popped in to check my post box and found a little note telling me I had a parcel. This would probably be the new bra I had ordered on the Internet, so I took the note into the main post office. Unfortunately, I had missed the parcel collection time and would have to go back next morning. So I continued home. I was tired when I got back, so I checked the pedometer my daughter had given me for Christmas. I had walked nearly five miles that afternoon, and that seemed to be fairly average for a normal day for me. I might be getting fitter, but my clothes told me I was not getting any slimmer! However, I realised that my irritable hip, which used to cause me endless discomfort, appeared to have resolved, so much so that I had forgotten all about it. A five-mile walk would have caused me considerable difficulty before, and I was now doing it on a daily basis with no problem. Possibly the warmth and the lack of humidity had something to do with it, but the "why" didn't really matter to me, as long as the end result was this pleasing!

February

As I walked to the post box the day following the president's visit, I noticed that he had been shielded from the unsightly building work. All the parts of the town that were still undergoing work had been hidden by large fabric covers, which made quite a decorative montage. Behind them were piles of rubble and scaffolding. A taxi driver recently told me that, whilst it was all right for the Luxor residents to stumble through the dust and rubble, it wouldn't do to let the president see all that. I had also been told that, in addition to the hundreds of military personnel lining the streets, there were probably thousands of plain-clothes security patrolling the town whilst he was here. I *had* seen a man with a Rotweiller on a tight lead near the museum, and I subsequently discovered that Condoleezza Rice was also with the president. No wonder security had been tight!

However, now everything was returning to normal, and the banners were slowly being removed as Luxor continued its day-to-day life. And I continued with my own. I returned to the post office to collect my parcel, and whilst there, I found another little note in my box. I took the two, and as I neared the main parcels office, I heard someone call good morning to me. As this was quite common, I didn't respond until I realised that it was the man who was normally in the post box room. He explained to me in Arabic that if I collected my first parcel, he had the second one in his office—at least, I thought that was what he was saying!

I went to see the usual lady in the parcels office. She offered me her tea, and I thanked her but declined. She immediately opened her drawer and got out a mandarin. Oh, no hurry then, you carry on and have your orange! However, my uncharitable thoughts were ill founded, as she opened up the mandarin and gave me several segments, insisting that I eat them! This Egyptian hospitality was something that always amazed me. I hoped that her hands were clean, and not wanting to offend, I dutifully ate my mandarin segments under her watchful gaze. She located my parcel, and I signed for it and paid the required 80p. I never did understand why one had to pay for parcels, but it seemed that was always the case. I went back to the post box to find the man who was holding my second parcel. He retrieved it for me, and again I signed, but there was no fee this time. This was great—a second Christmas!

I decided to call in at the duty-free shop on the way home and buy some wine. Although it is only possible to buy European spirits within forty-eight hours of arriving in Luxor, one can buy Egyptian liquor from the same shop anytime. In my limited experience, there was only one local wine that is drinkable, and this I purchased and carried on homeward bound. It was then that I made an impulsive buy! In the government shop, they had a set of blue glass bowls—six small and one large, which had reduced prices. I went in to look; At £5 for the set, it would be a pity not to buy them, really! I emerged with my parcel and headed swiftly for home, before I spent any more money!

My story of leaking gas at Christmas had frightened Mr. F. no end, and he was most diligent in his search for an electric cooker for me. I had been looking myself to no avail, but Mr. F.'s son had managed to locate one for me. I was thrilled, and so, I think, was Mr. F.! I was terrified of the bottled gas here; in the extreme heat of summer, the bottles were known to explode. Most weeks there was some terrible accident, and stories of whole buildings being blown up by a gas bottle were too common for comfort. I hopefully awaited more news about my new electric cooker.

I had also been thinking about my bedroom. My square mattress, perched on top of the circular one, gave a Princess-and-the-Pea-type effect. It was amazingly comfortable, but impractical, and it took up most of the floor space. I decided that if the circular bed were removed and the surround behind it cut back, the square bed could be put on a new frame and slotted back against the wall, thus lowering it and increasing the space in the room. Unfortunately, this would also entail laying new carpet, as it had been cut around the circular bed. I would talk to Mr. F. next time I saw him and see whether he could get a price for me. Similarly, in the spare bedroom, the beds were tucked underneath a book-shelf, which was precarious for the sleeper below, should they sit up suddenly! The removal of the lowest shelf would instantly solve the problem.

None of this could be done, of course, without funds, and I found to my enormous despair that once again my rent money from the UK was not forthcoming. I had been checking my bank account daily on the Internet and even allowing clearance time; this month's rent was overdue. It was a nightmare and became a real worry at the end of a month when there was nothing left in the kitty. I was re-gretting my purchase of the blue bowls and the wine, as I now only had 50 LE—about £5—left in my purse, and that was it until the next rent payment went in. My weekly shop would have to be postponed and so, for that matter, would everything else. My only alternative was to with-draw money from the ATM using my credit card, but I was reticent to do this as it incurred charges, and I would be robbing Peter to pay Paul.

I wrote yet another email to my agents, chasing payment. In addition, my neighbour back in the UK had emailed to say that the burglar alarm was going off at my flat, so I sent another email to the agent to suggest they investigate, turn it off, and reset it. Their reply came a few hours later. They had investigated and turned the alarm off, but they had not reset it. This was not good news. If the alarm was not set, my house insurance was invalid. I sent a third email to the agents, explaining this and informing them that they would be responsible for any theft or damage whilst the alarm was not set and asking them to confirm once this had been done. Why, oh why, was everything in England such a fight? Yes, things went wrong in Egypt, and yes, it was frustrating, but people came out swiftly to mend or replace, always with a smile and always for little money. It might take a second visit to get it done properly, but it was always done. I don't think I've ever had to badger and chase and complain the way I had to in England, and on top of all the hassle, it always cost a fortune. And people asked me why I had decided to live in Egypt?!

The next morning brought the blissful peace of Egyptian Fridays. I got up in my dressing gown and watched as a gate in the wall opposite was bricked up. One man was laying the bricks, another passing them to him, and a third bringing the bricks to the spot. It was done in no time, and then another man appeared to render the new wall. He administered the concrete solution and three men watched him—no change from England there! When this was completed, I watched as he put red paint on his rendering to match the existing wall. He had a large, flat bowl in which he put red powder before adding copious quantities of water. He then administered this to the wall by way of an old paint pot—not a brush in sight! A fourth man now appeared to watch the proceedings. He carefully added paint over the splashed areas of concrete, and the job was finished.

I wondered what was planned for this empty area, as there had been much activity there the day before, and at about 9:30 in the evening, several men had taken the double gates off another opening and had taken a mallet to one of them. I was never too sure why, and in the morning, the gates were back up in their normal place. I hoped they weren't going to start another building, but I rather supposed that they might.

I had been agonizing over my hair for several weeks. Despite valiant efforts to let the colour grow out and discover what my real colour now was, I was beginning to feel dowdy and considerably more than middle-aged. In the height of despondency, I bit the bullet and went into the hairdressers for a tint and a cut. They asked what colour I would like. Goodness, I didn't know! What were the choices? They showed me a swatch of different colours, and together we chose one. To say I was terrified is probably an understatement. After all, most Egyptian women are dark haired; did they actually know what they were doing with fair hair?

I watched with horror as a very white solution was put all over my head—this was not the colour I was used to seeing my UK hairdresser use! Neither was it carefully sectioned and applied; it was heaped on in large quantities and then massaged in. My heart was now in my boots. However, the end result was brilliant and almost identical to my usual colour. The cut was excellent, and I returned home feeling like a new woman! It was also cheaper than I had anticipated, which was just as well, considering my current financial crisis. Once more, my flexible friend provided sterling service!

The news on my cooker was not good. I was told I would find such a thing nowhere in Egypt. However, Mr. F. told me to go to the duty-free shop, where I could find an electric oven. He had located a two-ring electric hob. Off I set to find the said oven. It was slightly smaller than a split-level oven and clearly meant to be built into kitchen units. By Egyptian standards it was fearfully expensive, but it was exactly what I needed, so I went ahead.

My rent money had at last materialized, but I would need to use a credit card to cover the cost of the oven. Of course, like almost everywhere else in Luxor, it was not possible to use a card, so I trotted off to the nearest cash point. It declined my card. I went on to the next bank and tried again And encountered a similar problem. Finally, I went into the bank. A man came out to the machine with me, and we put my card in three times to get smaller amounts than I needed, incurring commission charges with each request. Finally, it refused to give any more, and I had to go back to the original ATM with a different card to get the balance. This was infuriating, as there were insufficient funds in that particular account, which meant I had to go back to the Internet and move money around. Finally, with a fist full of small notes making up the amount required, I returned to the shop to make my purchase. All went well until I came to discuss delivery. I had rung Mr. F. in the interim and arranged for the usual man to collect the oven and bring it home for me, but the shop were not used to this sort of arrangement, and it took yet another call to Mr. F. before they would accept it.

An hour later, my oven was delivered. I was in a complete panic over the amount I had spent, but I knew it was a good investment.

A few days later, Mr. F.'s son arrived with a carpenter. I had drawn a little plan of the kitchen, indicating how I wanted to inset the cooker. He nodded sagely and started to measure. I wanted to move my fridge to the opposite side of the kitchen, as its current placement made it a tight squeeze to get in and out of the room, and it blocked four cupboards. By taking down a shelf and moving a table, the fridge could be located at the opposite end, thus freeing lots of space. The carpenter would cut the table and make a shelf on which I could stand the fan, and all would be well.

We turned our attention to the bedroom and the alterations to the bed. Again, I'd made a little drawing of what I would like. The carpenter kindly removed the shelves from the spare bedroom, and I awaited the price. Unfortunately, it was more than I had anticipated, but having over-spent on the oven, I was on a roll; I gave the go-ahead for the work to be carried out. The carpenter said he would start straight away, and that in about two weeks, it would all be complete. Despite the worry about paying for it, I was excited by the prospect of the improvements.

I met my next visitors at the airport and had a really wonderful week with them. These were two ladies who I had worked with several years ago. We didn't know each other extremely well when they arrived, but I felt I had made two really good friends by the time they left.

Neither of them had been to Luxor before, and they were anxious to see as much as possible. With the invaluable help of the Egyptian friend who had planned my trip to Minya, we put together an itinerary for them with a guide. I joined them on their trip to Abydos, as I had only been there once before and had had insufficient time to see everything. We had a lovely day and a longer stop than usual at the temple, which enabled us to see everything we wanted to.

On another occasion, we walked the length of the Souk with our Egyptian friend there for moral support. He said that the shopkeepers were calling out to him to hassle us for them! He found that as funny as we did, and fortunately for us, he did not comply with their wishes. We did stop a few times for my guests to make purchases, and it was a thoroughly enjoyable excursion with much less of a fight over prices than if we'd ventured down there alone.

As they left for their return to the UK, the next mailshot for the conferences went out, and my days were set to be punctuated with the work involved with that. When I had decided to come to Luxor, there were no plans for future conferences for 2007, but things had changed; so with the help of two stoic friends in England and the wonders of modern technology, the booking forms and letters swept across cyberspace and were dispatched to delegates. I would never be able to thank these two friends enough for all the work they put in to this project, which enabled me to carry on with it.

I had been having enormous difficulty with my computer, particularly the email system that I was forced to adopt, which meant that I had to go through the Internet, rather than direct to my mailbox. The introduction by my Australian friend to an Englishman living in Luxor, who worked with computers, had proved to be a wonderful find. He went to great lengths to sort things out for me, and everything was back up and running twenty-four hours before the mailshot went out. I still had some gremlins to sort out in my DSL connection, and Mr. F.'s son and his friend had already been back to help, but the problem still remained. I requested their return to try conquering the problem once and for all.

The continuing challenge of the plumbing still assaulted me. This time it was the cloakroom basin. It had always been slow to empty, but now it would not empty at all. I found the usual drain-clearing crystals that usually did the trick, but on this occasion they did nothing to help. I would need the plumber back yet again. I had gone past the stage of irritation with these things; one just had to accept it. This, after all, was Egypt. If one was persistent, the problem was always solved, and everyone was happy to help. I would ask Mr. F. to send the man again and hope that he could take the offending part to pieces, which was what I was sure it needed.

A chat with Mr. F. also revealed that a neighbour two floors down had been worrying. This man had been living away for most of the two years that I had owned my flat, but he had returned that week. Within days of arriving, he was complaining that my water pump was on all the time and was a fire hazard. Wait a minute—hadn't we been down this path before? Mr. F. suggested that I should put a "button" somewhere in the flat to activate the pump when I wanted water. I was a little aggrieved. I explained to him that I might as well turn it on and off at the fuse as before if that was the case, but I was certain that the pump was functioning properly. It was never on when I left the building or when I came in, and when I had a shower, I could hear the pump kick in as the water pressure increased. I could not understand why this neighbour thought it wasn't working. We decided that it was fine to leave it, with Mr. F. gaily saying that if the building burned down because of my pump, then it would be my responsibility. This did very little for my equilibrium, as it was a worrying thought, but my common sense told me that the pump was fine and working as it should. I suggested to Mr. F. that if the man was still worried, he should knock on my door, and we could discuss it. I suspected he never would.

I had a few days of feeling a little off colour and was craving a hot water bottle to hold on my tummy. I decided to put a small towel in the microwave to warm up and then hold against my tum. The first attempt was very successful. However, when I did the same thing again to re-warm the towel, I got distracted by the television and was only reminded of the towel by the smell of something burning! I rushed to the microwave and whipped the towel out just as it was beginning to smoke. I looked at it in horror. Six very large circular burns covered the towel. I plunged it into a bowl of cold water, at which point one of the burn marks turned into a large hole! How lucky I had been that it hadn't actually caught fire, and how silly I had been to do it in the first place! It brought back a memory of boil washing some flannels many years ago and catching fire to the saucepan when I forgot about it! Necessity may be the mother of invention, but common sense must always prevail!

I had another evening visit from the computer trio, and my DSL line seemed to be up to speed again. We had moved the whole terminal to another location and plugged it in to the first incoming phone line. The splitter I had been waiting so long for was now put into place, and my phone worked whilst I was online. Excellent! However, the next morning I found I had no telephone at all; the line was completely dead, but with the computer line working, it was the least of my worries. I had my mobile phone, and very few people knew the landline number. As it happened, Mr. F. rang me on my mobile to say he could not get through on the landline, so I related the sorry tale. He said he would try to get the engineer back to look at it. He had taken the phone socket completely to pieces, but as it was working when he left, I wondered whether it was just a loose connection. I would wait until he came.

That morning saw the arrival of a different plumber for my cloakroom basin. I hadn't really thought about it before, but it struck me that morning that all the tradesmen arrived with their tools carefully placed in black plastic bags. This man was no exception, and he set to, to empty the water standing in the basin. He indicated that a plunger was needed, and I told him that I didn't have one. I showed him the clearing crystals that I had been using and tried to explain that they no longer did the trick, and that I thought the problem was lower down the pipe. He nodded sagely and got out his spanners. Ten minutes later, he showed me the waste pipe and the contents he had emptied from it. Rather like the water boilers, the pipe had been full of sludge and grit, just as I'd expected. He asked me for 10 LE to get something he needed, then returned with some mastic. He soon had the job finished and explained that I should not use the basin for six hours or I would have water all over the floor. He finished by asking for a cloth, with which he cleaned the whole floor. When I asked how much I owed him, he asked for £1.50. I was delighted all the more so because the job had been successfully completed before the arrival of my next visitors.

My anticipated new oven didn't bring the same joy. The carpenter arrived with a rather negative looking man—most unusual for Egypt. I thought they were there to measure the new hob, but the carpenter told me there was a problem. The oven had vents at the side, and if he encased it in a wooden cabinet, it would catch fire. I explained that it was designed to be encased in something, and he acknowledged that that was so in my country, but not in Egypt. I suggested that perhaps he could leave the sides open instead of building it into a cupboard. He was happy with this idea and suggested he could match the granite worktop to go over the top. I would, of course, then have to have the little two-ring hob sitting on the top, rather than built in. Disappointed that I could not reproduce what I had imagined, I reluctantly agreed and wondered what sort of dust trap I was making for myself with the two sides open. There seemed to be an obsession with fire risks here, and in a land of non-existent health and safety, it gave me cause to wonder—especially as I had been tripping through builders' rubble on the stairs for weeks, which really *was* a safety issue!

Next we went on to my bedroom, and the gloomy accompanist was talking incessantly in Arabic. He then opened my bedside drawer—excuse me! His friend leaned across my freshly laundered and newly made up bed. I groaned inwardly. Last time he came to measure, he'd left biro marks and grubby finger marks on the duvet cover. At least here, there didn't seem to be a problem, just a confirmation of what was to be done. When I inspected after they left, I found the linen still pristine!

I wondered what on earth I was going to end up with, and my confidence had a further wobble when the same carpenter said he would come and look at my telephone problem the next day. He had asked if he could come back at 10:00 p.m. that night, and I said no, it was far too late. They were all amazed, but he agreed to come at 2:00 p.m. the following afternoon instead. The Egyptian custom of sleeping all afternoon and staying up until the early hours of the morning was one that I found hard to adopt, and the thought of somebody trying to fix my phone line when I would usually be going to sleep was not one I could encompass. I just hoped he knew what he was doing with telephones and didn't interrupt my hard-fought computer line. If I couldn't get online, I would be lost. Ah well, I'd try to stay positive and keep my fingers crossed!

I went back to the computer to email, and despair began to grip as I experienced the same problems as I'd had all along. I was irked to pay a monthly subscription for a service that didn't function properly 50 percent of the time. I knew the computer crew would come back with the same goodwill I had experienced all along, but I would just like to get it to work consistently!

Feeling a little down from the day's events, I made myself some pasta and a tomato salad, hastily followed by some stiff brandies. The DVD I picked was a bad choice and reduced me to tears, so I cut my losses and went to bed early.

The following day started with a brisk walk to the post box and the baker with a coffee on the way, I returned to base in preparation for my next set of visitors. Two o'clock came and went, and there was no sign of the chaps for the phone line. They eventually arrived at 5:00 p.m.! After an hour of taking wires in and out, they decided an electrician was needed to check the whole system. This got better and better! The electrician was arranged to come the next day.

Fortunately, the computer was still functioning, and when checking my email, I found that my visitors' flight had been delayed by two hours. I wondered how I was going to check the new ETA. Come, come, I coached myself, I was an intelligent woman; I could do this! And I did do it, but it took me three hours! The airline they were flying with had no information on their website about flight arrivals and departures. Manchester Airport's website had listed the departures, but not the exact times. I knew their flight had left, but I didn't know *when* it had left. I tapped in Luxor Airport, and to my amazement a website materialised. They were showing the original ETA, which I knew wasn't correct anymore. I found a "contact us" button and sent off a rather tongue-in-cheek email. I then texted some friends in the UK to see if they could find out the departure and arrival information for me. Whilst they were diligently searching for me, to my absolute wonderment, an email came in from Luxor Airport giving me the exact ETA. How completely unexpected! I rang the taxi driver and rearranged the time, then managed to contact the man who would carry the bags up to the flat to change his time also. Unfortunately, he had already arrived outside, but seemed quite happy to come back later.

I arrived at the airport, but still had an hour to wait. You are not allowed inside at Luxor Airport, and the information board is inside. The only way to see it is by standing on one leg and squinting through the glass. If you are very lucky, you can just make out half the information board. I got chatting with another English lady who was collecting someone, and it helped to pass the time. She was very envious when my visitors arrived before hers and we set off happily for home.

The next few days passed in a routine of time at home, shopping, coffee with friends, and my visitors undertaking gentle trips that we had arranged for them. The weather was changeable: cloudy and cool one day, quite warm and sunny the next, but always at a manageable temperature to get chores done and walk anywhere.

I had had terrible problems trying to find a serrated knife to cut bread. Such a thing just didn't seem to exist. I had tried many places and even resorted to drawing in one shop. Ah-ha! A light of recognition appeared across the man's face. Then he took the pen from my hand and carefully crossed out the zig-zag edge of the knife I had drawn, proudly producing a straight-edged knife! Eventually, my Egyptian friend said he would find one for me, and I happily agreed to let him.

It had never occurred to me that the trees would lose their leaves at any time of the year other than October and November. But as I watched them fall in February, I realised that the leaves here probably fell as it got hotter, rather than as it got colder. I could now see the Nile again from my bedroom window. The leaves seemed to be falling from the top of the trees, with the bottoms retaining more foliage. The big buds that would eventually form exquisite, bright-red blooms covered the trees from top to bottom; a couple were flowering already. I remembered from previous visits that they were in fuller flower by May and June.

I returned from a visit to Mr. F. one evening and found that my current visitors from England had had a bad evening. On returning from their day out, the lady had fallen at the entrance to the building. I was pleasantly surprised to hear that three passers-by had rallied round, together with the man from the ground floor flat, who had offered a chair and any assistance required. Fortunately, it was not a serious fall, and a little first aid when they got back to the flat solved the problem. I hastily put some ice cubes to freeze to aid her swollen lip and was delighted when there were no serious repercussions the following morning.

My visitors had planned alternate days of excursions, and on one particular evening, we all ventured across on the passenger ferry with our Egyptian friend for dinner opposite the temple at Medinet Habu. Nobody else was there, and the dinner had been prepared just for us. It was typical Egyptian fare, including stuffed pigeon for the meat eaters, stuffed cabbage leaves, various vegetable tagines, and of course, ta-hini and bread. We had a thoroughly enjoyable evening.

I also joined them on a visit to the Ramasseum and Seti I Temple one morning. We got home in plenty of time for the carpenter, who had arranged to come at 3:00 p.m. to fit the new oven and my new bed. I cleared my bedside cupboards that were going to be taken out, but a sixth sense stopped me from stripping my bed. At 5:00 p.m., I rang to find out what time the carpenter would be coming and was told that it would be tomorrow at 3:00 p.m.! Lucky the bed was still made, then!

Next morning, I folded up my duvet and decided I would leave it at that, just in case! I went down to the bank and to buy a top-up card for my mobile, bravely walking through the new bazarre as a shortcut. I had avoided this like the plague previously, as in its former guise, I couldn't walk a step without someone pouncing on me, keen to get me into their shop. However, the new building was very smart, and although all the traders were sitting outside their shops, few of them even spoke as I passed. A few said good morning, and one asked if I wanted to look in his shop, but other than that, I walked through without incident—what an improvement!

I returned home to find the motor for the water pump was yet again failing to turn off. I turned the key in the lock, optimistically hoping that my visitors were running a shower or using the washing machine, but no such luck. I rang Mr. F., asking if he could send the plumber again. He told me it was very dangerous like this, so I assured him that I had turned it off at the fuse box. He asked again if I wanted a button to turn the water on and off, but I explained that I couldn't see why this was necessary, as I could turn it on and off at the fuse box. What I really wanted was a pump that worked properly all the time. Oh dear, he wasn't very happy with me, and I really didn't want to upset him. I suspect that dust gets into the motor and stops the switch from cutting out. I would endeavour to find out from other friends who lived here whether the "button" method was common, or whether I was right to pursue a properly working model.

We had great excitement that afternoon: it was the day of the new bed and oven! Mr. F.'s son arrived punctually at 3:00 p.m. to dismantle the circular bed. My bedding sat draped over a chair in the lounge as he took apart the structure. The little man who carried the suitcases arrived with his donkey and cart and single handedly carried everything down the stairs and loaded it up. The donkey was so small and his load so enormous, I wondered if he would ever be able to pull it. He stood there, oblivious to the world, eating whatever he could find on the ground.

Next a white pickup truck arrived with the new bits on it. A young boy came to help carry things, starting with the spare gas cylinder. He looked about twelve but was probably nearer nineteen. He was shaking with the exertion of it. I found my small money disappearing in leaps and bounds: 20LE for the driver of the van, 10LE for the boy, 50LE for the man doing the bulk of the carrying and so on. Watching them carry the old gas cooker was torture. Three of them lifted it on to one man's back! Surely he would never manage four flights of stairs like that! I watched over the balcony and saw three of them carry it to the cart, so hopefully it was a three-man job down the stairs!

Several hours of activity followed. The new bed was excellent with one exception: the bedside tables obscured the wardrobe doors. We all looked and we all scratched our heads, and eventually the carpenter said he would take them back and try and make them smaller.

The oven was a huge success. It looked excellent, and having the fridge at the opposite end of the kitchen made the room look twice as big. The carpenter had managed to match up the granite worktop exactly, despite a moment of difficulty when it was a bit too big. He shaved it down to size, and the finished result was wonderful.

Another two men made an appearance during the course of the evening: the electrician because the power point was faulty, and a man to cut the original glass top to the bed surround. More small notes evaporated from my purse!

They eventually left at 10:00 p.m., and I set to cleaning up the worst of the debris. They had done a very good job of clearing up themselves, but there was no way I could start breakfast in the morning unless I had cleaned the kitchen first that night.

At lunchtime the next day, the man with the donkey arrived to carry the offending bedside tables back to the carpenter. His delightful donkey waited patiently. I was now having to borrow small notes from my visitors to cope with the never-ending tipping! I wasn't too sure what to expect on Monday when these cabinets were coming back, but hopefully there would be a big improvement!

There was more excitement to come before Monday dawned. On Sunday night, I decided to make a lasagne to try out my new oven. All was going well. I was preparing the sauce on the hob and decided to turn on the oven so that it reached the correct temperature. Two minutes later, I was plunged into darkness! Fortunately, only the kitchen and bathroom were without power, so I optimistically went to the fuse box. Ah yes, there was the rogue fuse. I turned it back on and returned to the kitchen, fully expecting all to be well. Not so. Total darkness remained. This was fast becoming a Mr. F. situation! I rang him and explained. He told me he would send the electrician immediately.

Five minutes later, he rang back. The electrician was a Christian; this being Sunday, he had the day off and was with his wife at his mother-in-law's house just outside Luxor. However, he had a motorbike, and he would be with me within half an hour! Sure enough, about twenty minutes later he appeared on my doorstep. He spoke to Mr. F. and then went to the fuse box. A few minutes later, we had power. He then turned on the hob—bang!—darkness. He worked his magic again, and I rang Mr. F. for translation. He said I couldn't use the hob tonight, but I could use the oven, and he would be back at ten o'clock the next morning with some new parts. I thanked him profusely, and off he went. I returned to my lasagne, completed it, and put it in the oven. After two minutes—bang!—darkness again. I couldn't possibly leave it until the next morning, as my freezer was full and there was no way of getting it to a plug that worked.

I rang Mr. F. No problem, he said, he would ring the electrician and send him back. I had visions of this poor man answering his mobile whilst riding his motorbike, desperately trying to get back to his family. Ten minutes later he returned, a big grin on his face. He went to the fuse box and then to the kitchen. By this time, when I had pulled the plug out of the wall, I had also pulled the socket out! He expressed surprise, but he set to and put it back together again. I expressed by pantomime that I would not use the oven tonight, but he insisted it was fine. We plugged it in and waited—bang!—darkness again! He returned to the fuse box. We waited again. "All is good," he told me confidently before he left for the second time. I did not share his optimism, but my pessimism was ill founded, as all was well. I ate my lasagne, which by now had lost its appeal, and fervently hoped that he could put in a bigger fuse in the morning.

He did come the following morning. In a matter of minutes, he and his trusty assistant—who as far as I could tell did nothing more than hold up the lid of the fuse box—had put in the new wire. However, later that day a phone call from Mr. F. informed me that the whole fuse box needed to be replaced. The previous owner had hardly spent any time in the flat, and I had now installed a lot of electrical devices. The fuses were just not man enough for the job and needed to be replaced at a cost of 700LE. I was not surprised. The lights that switched themselves between one bulb, two, or rarely, three, were a dead giveaway! The electrician would come on Wednesday to do the job and to look at the rogue water pump.

In the meantime, the carpenter who was replacing the bedside tables kept putting off his appearance on a daily basis. He, too, I was told, would now come on Wednesday with the electrician. Well, I would believe that when I saw it!

Wednesday dawned, and the electrician returned. He completely rewired the fuse box and addressed all the non-working lights. He left after about three hours with everything working as it had never done before—even the water pump! However, I was warned not to run things like the dishwasher and the washing machine at the same time.

The carpenter arrived in the afternoon with two miniature bedside tables. With a little persuasion, they fitted superbly into the gap on each side of the bed and were exactly what I had wanted. I was delighted. The carpenter expressed doubt as they were so small, but I assured him that they were perfect.

Such perfection never seems to last long in Egypt. Within a week, I discovered a huge leak from the bathroom toilet. The plumber was dispatched via Mr. F., and a new pipe was purchased and installed, all for a total of 30LE and a total time of about half an hour. My equilibrium now restored, daily life recommenced. But within twenty-four hours, I found a leak in the other toilet. I couldn't believe it! Back came the plumber; incredulously, the same fault had appeared in this toilet as in the other one. He returned the next day with another new pipe and quickly had the problem solved. He asked for 20LE this time, but as I only had a 50 and he had no change, I decided it was worth the 50. He was very reluctant to take it, but I assured him it was all right, and off he went.

The only thing remaining to be sorted was the new electric hob. This had a fault, despite being new: the large burner came on when you plugged it in, its switch not working. The electrician had taken it apart and tried to rewire it, but it still came on with the plug and was either on or off with no gradation. I asked Mr. F. if I could return it to the shop for a replacement. He said he thought it was unlikely, but that we could try. Ah, this looked decidedly doubtful. I arranged with him that I would take it down to his office at the end of the week, and we would go to the shop to see what they said.

In the aftermath of all this, I decided I was long overdue for a haircut, so I took myself down to the usual place the next morning. Yet again, I had a completely different hairdresser who I'd never seen before. How many did they have? I'd presumed they worked on a rotation basis round the hotels, but perhaps they just had a high turnover! As always, I ended up with a variation on my desired cut, but it was well cut and would resurrect when I washed it myself. The girls, who seemed always to be the same group, persuaded me to have a manicure and pedicure. Feeling a little shell shocked after all the recent goings-on, I decided I would treat myself. I came home with bright pink toenails and pale pink fingernails, both with little flower decorations. There was nothing like a bit of pampering to put the spring back in your step.

My previous visitors having left on Monday afternoon, I spent much of the week washing, ironing, and cleaning, in preparation for the next visitor the following Monday.

Life was becoming more routine the longer I stayed, peppered with delightful interludes and sightseeing with my visitors. My happiest morning since my arrival was spent with a friend, walking from the Valley of the Kings over the mountain to the Valley of the Queens. In distance, it wasn't very far, but the initial climb was quite steep, and the paths were full of rubble. Halfway along the route we passed the remains of the workers' huts, where they used to stay if they did not want to return from working in the Valley of the Kings all the way back to the village. It was a lot bigger than I had anticipated and very atmospheric. You could almost see the ancient workers, returning here after hours of working in the tombs. At the top the whole panorama of the valley floor below opens up, and you can see all the mortuary temples. The complete quiet contrasted with the hustle and bustle of the Nile Valley. The experience was completely magical. We stayed for a while, then carried on past the workers' village to the Shrine of Ptah, where again we stopped for a few moments. As we went into the small cave, I was anxious that there might be snakes, but I didn't see any. We continued down to the Valley of the Queens, where the car met us.

We finished off with a leisurely lunch at Africa, a café on the West Bank, then made our way home. It was a perfect day, summarising all that Luxor meant to me.

March

I ventured down to Mr. F. by taxi with the rogue hob. Although we had arranged to meet at 7:00 p.m., he was not there, and the office was closed. I rang his mobile phone and there was no reply. I waited. Ten minutes later he arrived, full of apologies. His secretary had left that week, so there had been nobody to open up the office. I sat for nearly an hour whilst he saw to phone calls and visitors. Then his son arrived, and together we went down to the shop with the little hob.

There was clearly a problem with the fact that I was returning it. The man at the shop was reticent to do anything about it. I sat, trying to look demure, whilst raging inside; if this were England, it would just be replaced! However, this was *not* England, and as I had chosen to live here, I had to accept the Egyptian way of doing things. I had to face it: the guarantee I had wasn't worth a light, and there was no way this was going to be replaced, only repaired. Since the electrician had been unable to repair it, I felt less than optimistic. However, we left the hob in the shop, and Mr. F.'s son said he would collect it and deliver it for me the next day. I really couldn't ask for more.

I had awakened with a dreadful headache that morning, possibly the result of Egyptian wine, which seemed to have that effect on me! I decided I wouldn't buy any more and would stick to my brandy or Pimms. That said, tonight would definitely be alcohol free; the thought of an early night was most appealing.

There was no sign of the hob the following day, but it was Sunday, and many of the Christian-owned shops were closed. Monday evening came, and Mr. F.'s son rang to say he was bringing the hob to me. We took it into the kitchen and plugged it in. He proudly showed me that the light now came on, and I saw that the switch had been altered. There were traces of glue round the knob, and it was slightly proud now, but yes, the light did come on! After he had gone, I experimented to see whether the large ring still came on with the smaller burner, but it was impossible to tell, since it was now hot already. I stoically decided to leave it until the next day, and if it was still troublesome, I would have to replace it.

I had been watching the little birds in the trees opposite. I thought when I'd been here previously in March that the flowers on the trees were just starting to open, but I realised now that they opened in February, and that by March they were beginning to fade. At the moment, they were in full flower, and the effect was glorious: bright red, lily-type flowers with long stamens. Everywhere I looked were small sparrow-like birds, flocking to the flowers and sipping the nectar. At the top of the taller tree was a large nest. Much bigger birds frequented it, and I watched in awe as wind made the branches sway, wondering with amusement whether baby birds got seasick!

I had spent the day tidying up for my next visitor. Cleaning was always very satisfying if I had left it for a few days, as I could actually see where I had been in the dust! I looked around the flat with satisfaction: it was spic and span. I still had several hours to wait before I went to the airport, so I settled down with a drink and the television. The car arrived, and I got to the airport in plenty of time, collected my visitor, and returned to the flat. We spent an hour or so chatting, and I went to bed at about 1:30 a.m.

The next day, with bated breath, I tried the little hob. To my intense joy and, I have to say, some amazement, I found that it worked! The two rings heated independently, and the larger ring remained off until switched on! I suspected it was either on or off, with no gradation, despite the fact that it had four different settings—but hey, on or off was good!

On my visitor's second day, we went down to the orphanage. This particular orphanage is a registered British charity, which was started by an English woman who was distraught by the amount of children she saw on the street. She set up the basis of the home for four children, and they now have seventy-three! They have recently acquired a second building, and this was my first visit to their new abode.

I was feeling very guilty, as I sponsor a little girl there and had not managed to visit her in all this time living in Luxor. She is three and a half and never remembers me from one visit to the next. She is very shy, but still naughty on the quiet! Today was a good breakthrough, as she came and held my hand, but not for long—and then she made it quite clear that she had had enough, pulling away and busying herself with other things! She had grown such a lot since I had last seen her and was looking very pretty with her dark curly hair and purple shirt.

We were shown all over the new premises, which were delightful. The whole top floor was an outdoor play area—a wonderful facility for these children, who had always had to play inside before. We played with the children, cooed over the babies, and cuddled so many who wanted to be picked up and loved.

The smaller toddlers were up on the rooftop play area, and one little girl wanted to be cuddled continuously by the English lady who was giving our tour. They had a wonderful selection of playthings: a ball pit, a slide, swings, playhouses and tents, and a pet tortoise. Half the area was under cover— ideal for the hot Egyptian sun. The two-to-four-year-olds were in the kindergarten area. Here they had an English room, an art room, and a play area, and they rotated in groups around the three. These children loved to see visitors and asked to be picked up. I always have to watch my bag, as they love to undo zips. Today a fellow visitor found a little boy carrying my letter, which had been in my bag ready for posting! I retrieved it gratefully and popped it quickly back into my bag!

We left after an hour and a half, having spent such a happy time with the beautiful children. I was full of admiration for the achievement of building the new premises.

Of course, not every day is perfect in paradise. A time of personal problems made for a sleepless night and more than a few tears. Even the beautiful surroundings of the Nile, mountains, palm tress, and feluccas could not lift my mood. In fact I think it made it worse to see such beautiful things and such a beautiful place while I was feeling so down. As I neared the end of my Egyptian dream, it seemed important to remember the bad days as well as the good. I was sure that when I got back to the dull, overcast days of the UK, the financial worries, and the daily grind, my memories of Egypt would all be rose coloured. It seemed sensible then to record the fact that, here, too, there were hard days.

Determined not to wallow—having drifted around in my nightie for most of the morning, steadily working my way through a box of tissues—I resolved to shower, dress, and go out and immerse myself in something. Unfortunately, it was a day when there was nothing much I actually *needed* to do, and being Sunday, the shop that I really *wanted* to go to was closed. However, I would go down to the post box and the bookshop and then see how the day unfolded. It had always been my way in times of difficulty to fill every possible moment in a frenzy of keeping myself busy. It had always worked, so this would be my way forward today. Of course, having someone to stay was also a good thing, ensuring that I got on and kept busy and didn't get too bogged down with my problems.

A difficult few days followed, but my personal problems gradually resolved, and I began to perk up again. I emailed some friends in England who are involved in helping another charity in Luxor, a clinic for disabled children. They sent back a contact name and telephone number, and I rang to arrange a visit.

My visitor and I went there by taxi. The clinic was large, bright, and airy and everyone welcomed us with warm smiles. The manager of the clinic showed us around. It ran purely on donations: patients pay a little if they can afford to do so, but nobody was ever turned away; if they were unable to pay, their treatment was completely free. Many of the children there had cerebral palsy, but there were many different disabilities. There were also some adult patients. In addition there was a pre-school every morning and a clinic every evening. There was a dental surgery and an operating theatre, and all the staff are volunteers. This wonderful place was achieving amazing results. I asked whether they could use another pair of hands and was delighted by how pleased they would be for my help. We came away overwhelmed by what we had seen.

My visitor's ten-day stay seemed to fly by, and soon she was off to the airport again. I looked around the flat. It seemed very quiet, but worse, the dust was incredible! We had had two days of really gusty wind, and, as always, this brought dust and sand in by the bucketful! I was told that this was the time of year for the *Khamsin*, and stupidly, I had left the windows open to blow what I thought would be "fresh air" through. All it achieved was blowing half the desert through! It was beyond polish and duster, and I set to with a bowl of water and a cloth. I didn't think I would ever get over the amount of dust here. I did half, and then, crippled with a headache, I went to bed with some migraine tablets. I couldn't sleep, so I got up tentatively and continued the chores. The headache was still there in the background. Some gentle ironing seemed a good idea until I burned my hand on the iron! Perhaps I would go out for a breath of fresh air instead!

I walked across the road and down a side street to the electrical shop. I had decided that I needed to rethink my bedroom. It wasn't hot enough for air-conditioning yet, but the nights were very warm. What I really needed was a ceiling fan. This would be impossible with the bedroom's present format, as there was a central ceiling light. The way forward would be to replace this with a fan and then find some wall lights. I arrived at the shop and found something that would fit the bill: a wall lamp in the shape of a lotus flower on a wooden surround. I bought two and two light bulbs for a total of £27, which seemed very reasonable. I had spoken to Mr. F., and he was going to arrange for the electrician to come and see to this for me. I was pleased with my purchases and looked forward to the changes.

The wind continued into the third day, although not as strong. I watched as some of the birds caught the air currents and hovered on the spot over the branches of the tree opposite. The remaining leaves had been blown completely off the trees now, and my lovely view of the Nile was now almost uninterrupted. I stood at my bedroom window and watched two large Nile cruisers. This was going to be very, very hard to leave behind.

After breakfast, I wandered down to a shop that was making some blouses for me. I had taken two of my favourites in to be copied, and I was thrilled with the results; they were absolutely perfect. I did find a dirty mark right in the front of the pale pink one. I pointed it out, and the man said he would wash it out for me. If that was not possible, they would remake it. I then chose some material for two pairs of trousers and arranged to return the following week to collect these and the pink blouse. I had managed to buy these four items for a little over the cost of one pair of trousers in the UK, so although it felt extravagant, I felt little need for justification.

I continued on to the photo shop, intending to have some prints done and to put all my photos onto a CD. To my horror, the memory stick was almost empty, with only one set of the photos I needed. There was no real need for panic, as all the photographs were loaded onto the computer; the only reason I wanted them on CD was because I was always afraid that the computer would crash and I'd lose everything. They printed what was on the memory stick and put them onto the CD, and I set off for home.

It was such a glorious day that I stopped at a riverside café on the way home for some soup and a coffee. I sat right beside the Nile in the sunshine, and a deep feeling of contentment filled me, wiping out the bad memories of the previous few days. There was something about Egypt that was balm for the soul.

There was also something about me and kettles, it seemed! I had owned the flat for two years, and in this period of time, I'd gone through three kettles! This morning saw the demise of yet another! I filled it with water, gasping for coffee, switched it on, and . . . nothing! I fiddled with the switch and found that it flickered on when I held it at a certain angle, but not for long. Clearly there was a loose wire, but the whole thing was a sealed unit. Resolving to buy another, I poured the water into a saucepan and put that on the hob. Whilst waiting, I switched on my computer. I went back and checked the water and returned to the computer. Twenty-five minutes later, I had checked and answered all my email, and the water was still not boiling! So much for the repaired ring on the hob! It was hot, but it seemed to switch itself off once it got to a certain degree of heat, so the water was never going to boil. I turned on the smaller ring, but of course it was going to take a few minutes to warm up. By now, my need for coffee was reaching desperation point, but to my relief, the little saucepan was soon boiling and the coffee made.

After breakfast, I strolled down to the shop to buy a new kettle. A man was sitting on the counter, swinging his legs.

"Do you speak English?" I enquired.

"Oh yes," he replied, then called to a lady.

She came over.

"This lady speaks English," he told me.

He continued to sit on the counter, and she called to another chap once I had requested a kettle. He found one for me, got it out of the box, poured in some water, and boiled it to show me that it worked. I was pleased by this demonstration, especially after the rapid demise of the previous three kettles! He then wrapped the hot kettle back into its cellophane packing and put it back in the box.

"How much?" I asked.

"With the discount, 40LE."

In British currency, £4. This was good. At this price, I didn't really mind if it went the way of the others, but I still hoped vehemently that it lasted a little longer.

I took the kettle home and rang for a taxi. My weekly supermarket run was so much cheaper now that I was living on my own again. It was surprising how much extra it cost having visitors. Not being a big breakfast eater myself, I was surprised by how often I had to replenish things like butter and jam. Of course, drinking everything black and generally disliking milk, the amount of milk that my visitors consumed was truly amazing to me and had invariably caught me on the hop! This particular morning, I spent £12 in the supermarket and £2.20 on fruit and vegetables. The first weekly shop I did on my return to the UK was going to be a terrible shock to the system!

I checked my email again on my return, and it's a good thing I did so. My friend dealing with my post had forwarded a threatening letter from the company I had my broadband connection with. The tenants had not paid the last bill, and the broadband company was threatening to discontinue the connection. I was furious. Six weeks earlier, the agent had assured me that this bill would be paid. I had gone to enormous lengths to explain to the company that I was returning to the UK and that they should switch the account back into my name to ensure that the service was uninterrupted. In one fell swoop, all my endeavours seemed to have been in vain. I emailed the agent immediately and received a reply within five minutes. She could not understand why the service hadn't been paid and said she would look into it that morning. Somehow my confidence in this was thin.

Lack of communication appeared to be my current *bete noir*. Upon waking the next morning, I switched on the computer. Early mornings were generally the best time to get a faster Internet connection. However, this particular morning I could not get onto the system. By lunchtime I was still not connected, so I went down to the nearest hotel to try to check my email that way. I wished I hadn't bothered. It cost me £3 for half an hour, and although I could get to the website for my email, the inbox was empty. I treated myself to a Turkish coffee and returned home. Still no Internet. I texted the friend who had helped with my previous computer problems. The text did not go through. I rang and got his voicemail. Close to screaming point, I rang my German friend, intending to meet up for a little light relief. She was at home with her little boy who was unwell, so we couldn't meet up. What was it about me this morning? Everything I touched was going wrong, and I seemed destined to be alone today. Even the electrician had cancelled! This also irritated me, as he was supposed to install the ceiling fan in my bedroom and I had already stripped all the bedding.

Feeling more than a little morose, I poured myself a Campari and soda. I rarely had a drink at lunchtime; heavens, was I becoming an alcoholic?! I really needed to do something constructive, but I couldn't apply myself to anything. I had to check my email soon, as I was awaiting various replies on several wheels I had put into motion. Even the book I was reading did not hold my attention for long.

Perhaps some vigorous cleaning would do the trick. It was obviously going on two floors down—on my way out, I'd seen what looked like jumble sale on the landing. This was the usual way the flat's occupants did their cleaning. Nearly everything was emptied out onto the landing—carpets, rugs, and furniture—and then presumably they had a clear run through to sweep and wash floors. I had noticed it several times. The rest of us just had to manage as best we could to clamber through the piles on our way up or downstairs!

It was surprising how uncomfortable I now felt going out without being fairly covered up. I saw some of the tourists in their shorts, strappy tops, and flip-flops and almost found it as unacceptable as the Egyptians did! It suddenly seemed an odd way to be dressed when walking down the street, and I found myself wearing more and more when I went out. Even short sleeves seemed a bit risqué, and I was much happier if I could find a longer-sleeved blouse to go over a T-shirt. Of course, that made me much hotter, but some of my T-shirts had very short sleeves, and I felt quite uncovered in them now. I also preferred to wear a more closed-in sandal, as it made for easier walking. I certainly thought twice about where my destination would be if I wore a pair of three-quarter-length trousers. The realization that my perspective had changed this way had only struck me the previous day when I had decided to put a blouse over the top of what I was wearing. When and how did that happen?! I suppose it started because I attracted a lot less attention when more covered. I'd also developed a healthy respect for the local people and shared their horror at what some of the tourists felt was acceptable. I did not want to be labeled alongside the brazen tourist brigade!

Next morning, I still had no Internet connection. I packed my laptop up and walked down to the nearest Internet café. My jeweler friend stopped me to say hello and remarked that he had not seen much of me lately. I explained that I had had many visitors, which had kept me busy. I asked him about the Internet café, and he took me in and introduced me, explaining my problems to the owner of the café. The owner sat me down and got me connected to a wireless connection while my friend brought me a cup of mint tea. The DSL link was very fast, and in no time I had got my email—what a relief! I sat and replied to them, and just before I had finished, my phone rang. It was Mr. F., wondering where I was. The electrician was waiting at the flat! I said I would be there soon and hastily packed up the laptop. I asked how much I owed for my Internet session and was told 5LE—50p! I gave him 10LE, thanked him, and hurried back home.

I'd had no idea that the electrician was coming that morning. I arrived home to find him, his coworker, and Mr. F.'s son waiting outside the door. We all went in and work began installing my ceiling fan in the bedroom. We discussed the wall lights; he didn't think he could install them. So I asked if he could move the ceiling light to a different point in the ceiling, but he didn't think he could do that, either. Mr. F. rang. He said they would have to cut into the ceiling for the fan, and he wanted to know if that was all right. I replied in the affirmative, telling him that I could sort out the lights another day.

About fifteen minutes later, the fan was installed, and the electrician showed me how to work it. It functioned from a switch by the bed as well as one by the door. There were plenty of other lights in the room, so it would be fine for now. I paid them £16, and they left me with dust and bits all over the bedroom. Fortunately, I had hastily covered the bed with a dustsheet before they'd started, so all was well after a quick run round with the Hoover.

That afternoon, I decided on a little siesta, but sleep evaded me when another selection of personal problems invaded my consciousness. After an hour I gave up. I lay there thinking that I would get up, when there was an almighty crash just by my head. I sat bolt upright, my heart racing, and looked behind me. The ornate mirror that occupied the whole wall behind the bed had just fallen off the wall and broken! I couldn't believe it. When I looked, I realised that it had only been stuck on with glue and suspected that the vibration of the fan had probably caused the problem.

Feeling that my whole existence was somewhat cursed, I fetched the dustpan and brush. The majority of the glass was behind the bed, which was fixed in place. I checked that there was no glass in the bed and cleaned up as best I could.

An hour later, Mr. F. rang. He thought my Internet connection was lost because the payment for the DSL line had been late this month. The company would look into this later tonight, and hopefully it would be put right tomorrow. Nobody needed to come to the flat because I knew the computer wasn't the problem; after all, it had worked at the Internet café. I thanked Mr. F. for the information and told him about the mirror. He said he would arrange for a man to come at 10:00 the next morning to sort it out.

I was feeling a little bogged down by things. My mind was reeling with the various things I was trying to sort out, both in Egypt and back in the UK. There were big decisions I had to make, and now in my last few weeks of my "gap year," I had to face these things again. The decisions were more or less made, but there was a lot of heartache in the making them, and my stress levels were back to the level they were before I left the UK. I would have to seriously take myself in hand or I would end up with migraine, but this was easier said than done. It was at times such as these that I missed my friends the most. It was expensive to phone the UK, especially for the hour-long sort of conversation I was needing, and I couldn't just jump in the car and go visit. This was good character building, I told myself, just bite the bullet and get on with it!

Next day, shortly after 10:00 a.m., two men arrived to measure for the new mirror. They returned an hour later with a new one, functional but nothing like the ornate previous one. I left them to it, and it was up and fixed in no time. They put a small plinth at the bottom so that it could not fall the same way again. Unfortunately, I had forgotten to cover the bed this time, although I had stripped the bedding. I was not too pleased to find splinters of glass all over the mattress after they had gone. Out came the Hoover, and it was soon cleaned up. I Hoovered the floor diligently, hoping that I wouldn't have cut feet when I next ventured out of bed barefooted.

Half an hour later, the DSL engineer arrived. He couldn't understand the problem, although he could see that there was one. He returned to his office and rang me a short while later from there. I didn't know what he had done, but the problem was resolved, and I felt much relieved. I just hoped it would behave for the final six or seven weeks.

The museum kitchen remained a source of entertainment. The changes they made were never ending. Their current project was to put a grid of iron across the roof, and I wondered what the covering was for. Tables had appeared here; perhaps they were enlarging the restaurant, but nobody ever seemed to be out there except the kitchen staff. Unfortunately, it was a noisy operation with sawing and welding into the early evening, and I watched in horror one evening as a young man balanced on the roofing scaffolding whilst his colleague removed the ladder! Deciding this was much too stressful to watch, I walked away. When I next looked out, the place was deserted, so I presumed that all had ended well.

I finally managed to get a good night's sleep. I seemed to have come full circle; I remembered my sleepless nights when I first arrived, but that had been from excitement—now it was from concern. Having had a good night, I felt like a zombie the next morning—worse, in fact, than when I'd had no sleep at all! I decided on a visit to the hairdresser to perk me up.

Some of my funniest moments had been at this hairdresser, and this day was no exception. The hairdresser was one who had done my hair before, but I produced my photographs to refresh his memory, nonetheless. It became a work of art. Each strand was put into place with the aid of hairspray, and I resigned myself to the "crunch effect" of previous visits. By the time I had walked home in the breeze, I looked as though I had stuck my fingers into an electric socket. To say he had achieved "lift" was an understatement; my hair was standing on end! Not one to be daunted, I took the hairbrush to it and soon had it looking like something I recognised. I was fast becoming their best client, as I suspected most of their clientèle were one-off visits from hotel residents, and as such, I was now getting a 50 percent discount! It was a good ploy on their part, as it certainly encouraged me to go more often than I might otherwise have done.

I'd decided against the wall lights in my bedroom. The electrician had seemed to indicate that it would be a problem, so I took them back to the shop. Much discussion followed. The owner's policy was to exchange, not to refund. I tried to explain that I didn't need any more lights, so the manager was called. He told me the same, but I stuck with it. Finally, he said he would ask the owner. He returned swiftly, telling me I could have my money back. I thanked him and walked home.

As I was walking down the road, I spotted a fly wandering around the bald head of the man in front of me. He didn't seem to notice. How could he *not* notice? Surely it must tickle. I found myself riveted to his head and the fly. After some distance down the road, the fly altered its position to the man's forehead, and that was when he noticed it and swatted it away. I continued on my way home, my source of entertainment gone!

Walking down the Corniche the previous day, I had received the usual selection of offers—taxi, caleche, felucca—but as I neared my destination and was preparing to cross the road, someone called out, "Madame, you are very short!"

Did I hear that right? Short? Well, I'm five feet, five inches—not tall, but not short, surely? If I was short, that would make one of my daughters, at just over five feet, a dwarf! I decided not to react and continued, only to hear the next comment from someone different:

"You have a lovely figure!"

Oh, please, let's at least keep it within the realm of possibility!

Still chuckling to myself, I arrived at the shop that was making the trousers for me. I was taking them back because they had been too big, and I was collecting the blouse they had altered, because it had been too small! I tried on the blouse, which he said they had only altered by two millimeters. It was a much better fit, and I was pleased. I then tried on the trousers to indicate the problem. Everything was noted, and I was told to return in two or three days.

I made the usual supermarket run, then staggered up the stairs with my shopping mostly in my backpack, carrying my shoulder bag and a carrier of light things such as toilet rolls and kitchen paper. Halfway up, a neighbour was at her door. I said hello, but she called me back. There was another lady who lived in this household. I didn't know what their relationship was, but she seemed to have had a stroke; her speech was impaired, and she had a withered hand and a strange gait. To my horror, my neighbour indicated that this poor woman would carry some of my shopping for me. No, no, I thanked her, but they were both insistent. In desperation, I handed her the bag of light things, but their intention was for her to take the backpack. Now this was really heavy this week, and I couldn't possibly let this poor little lady carry it for me; in fact, I had visions of her falling straight over if she took it, so I tried to imply that it was really no weight at all. We progressed up the remaining two flights together. I reached for my purse by way of thanks, but she was adamant that payment was not necessary, so I thanked her again, and she returned to the flat below. I was touched by their kindness.

During the last few days of March, the weather changed dramatically, and it was now very hot. The ceiling fan in the bedroom had proved invaluable, and I now turned one of the air-conditioning units on in the sitting room in the evening. When I looked at the temperature in the early morning and late evening, it was still eighty-five to ninety degrees, so I guessed it must be tipping the one hundred in the afternoons.

Finding myself with no plans for a couple mornings, I decided to spend them at one of the hotel pools. The swimming pool was freezing! I stepped down into the water with my brain telling me, "no, no, do not do this," but with a traditional British stiff upper lip, I carried on and immersed myself, swimming rapidly to keep warm. The hotels all boasted heated pools, but in my experience, very few of them felt that way. It didn't take many strokes before I became acclimatised and I thoroughly enjoyed my dip. I returned to the sunbed and my book and enjoyed my lazy morning.

I stopped at the local shops on my way back to buy some incense, and the friendly computer man directed me to the right shop. I found some that I liked and asked the price.

"Anything you would like to give me, I will accept," I was told.

How I hated this. Whatever I suggested was going to be too low, and it would end up in a bargaining session just for two packs of incense. Eventually, I persuaded him to give me a price. Inevitably, it was high. He then said he would like to give me a present. I suggested that I would rather have a cheaper price than a present, especially as I lived in Luxor. Much to my delight, the price came immediately down by a third! It was going to seem strange when I got back to the UK to have to accept the ticket price on everything!

On returning home, I had a quick lunch and decided to make lasagne for my dinner before it got too hot in the kitchen to cook. All was progressing well until I reached for the packet of lasagne, which contained only three sheets of pasta! Ah, now this was going to prove an interesting lasagne! The local supermarket was closed today, as it was owned by Christians and today was a Sunday, and the lasagne certainly didn't warrant a trek anywhere farther afield. Ingenuity was required, clearly! I looked in my cupboards and pulled out some macaroni; I would just have to layer it up with that instead. This surely was one of the great bonuses of living alone: anything goes, and if it is disaster, there is nobody else to know!

April

April. Was it really April already? I was six months into my Egyptian Dream, and only five short weeks remained. I could hardly believe it.

After the previous days and nights of heat, I was awakened in the night by a banging door and realised that there was a wind again. It was a welcome relief in the night, and the next morning was beautiful. It was still hot, but the breeze made it more than comfortable, an absolute joy.

I called for a taxi and was collected at 10:00 a.m. The first stop was for wrapping paper, as I had been wrapping my gifts in scented shelf paper, unable to find anything conventional! I found exactly what I wanted, and we went on to the Vodafone shop. I wanted to know if I could change my SIM card so that I could still use the phone in the UK. It was possible, but a little complicated. I decided to put it on hold for now. I went next door to the fish shop and bought a huge bag of frozen prawns for £4. Then I went across the road to the household shop, where I found a new squeezy mop and, to my delight, some plates that matched the bowls I had bought. Delighted with my purchases, I went on to the fruit shop and the baker and finally the supermarket. At that moment, my phone rang, and it was the shop to say that my trousers had been altered and I could pick them up.

We returned to the flat, and I put my cold and frozen things away, then went back to the taxi. It dropped me off near the shop, and I went in to try the trousers. Sadly, they were still not right. Back they went into the plastic bag to be returned and altered again. Maybe this would be the lucky third time.

I walked back in the warm sunshine, enjoying every moment. Unfortunately, my joy was short-lived; I made a phone call to the UK enquiring about some funds I had released. I had sent a letter by DHL the previous week, and they'd promised a two-day delivery. A girl in the UK told me it had not been received, but she would check their post room and call me again the next day.

The next morning, I got up early and set off to the DHL office. There weren't many people about, and the temperature was wonderfully cool. I ambled down the Corniche beside the Nile, which immediately restored my peace of mind. When I got to the DHL office, I had to wait ten minutes for the senior man to arrive. As soon as he was there and I explained my problem, he got on the phone to check. Yes, my letter had been delivered in two days as they had promised; he gave me the name of the person who had signed for it. This was a relief, but still a worry. Where exactly had this letter disappeared to within this large organization? And why was it that, whenever there was a financial problem, the fly in the ointment was always at the English end? I was going to have to make another phone call and fight my corner, yet again.

I went back via the hotel to book a haircut and a colour. As before, they asked me what colour I would like. I looked at the selection and couldn't remember which one I had chosen before. I held the card up to my head, and two of the girls expressed their opinions. I offered up a little prayer and chose one, arranging to go in the next morning at 10:30 a.m. As I walked out, the hairdresser I'd had last time passed me and said good morning. I groaned inwardly. I had hoped they had done their usual change around; out of all the different hairdressers, this one, although quite charming, was the one I had the least faith in, as his results were the least pleasing. He would undoubtedly be the one on the rotation this week. This would be the third time he had done my hair. Oh well, nothing ventured, nothing gained!

I had a coffee at the hotel before I left, then popped into the local supermarket for some fruit juice and washing powder. Next I went to the pharmacy for nail varnish remover and talc. As I walked up the busy, dusty street, I realised just how much I was going to miss all this. I thought back to when I first arrived, and how walking down the street like this gave me a stiff neck, as I had rigidly tried not to look about me in an effort to avoid being hassled! I couldn't pinpoint when, but somewhere along the line I had just relaxed, got on with it, and accepted it as normal. This morning it was a pleasure, especially as I managed to get everything I needed.

Later that afternoon, I made my first visit to the clinic to help with the disabled children. It was a sobering experience. I was introduced to the doctor in charge of all the medical treatment. He explained to me the type of treatments they offered, suggesting I might like to help with the play therapy. This involved encouraging them to use their disabled limbs in play, such as passing a ball to another child or playing with water. He called all the other volunteers in and introduced me to them. There were five of them, and I had forgotten the first one's name by the time I got to the fifth! All five were in their late twenties, and delightful, friendly and welcoming, with ready smiles and an obvious companionship between them. We arranged for me to volunteer two afternoons a week, Tuesdays and Thursdays, and I was taken straight away into the play therapy area.

I met a little boy with cerebral palsy and his mother. This little boy was such a happy little chap, smiling and laughing all the time. Although he was five years old, he was so small and unable to stand. We put him across a foam wedge, which encouraged him to hold his head up to look at us or play with anything. He had no use of his left hand at all, which was clawed, but lots of toys had him smiling and laughing and trying to interact. His mother was an older lady who was very happy for me to step into this role. She sat back and watched. I wondered if this little lad was one of many and if this extra burden was really causing her to struggle.

After a while, the activity changed and we strapped the boy into a frame, which was then put upright, giving him the sensation of standing and strengthening his back and neck muscles. His poor little head kept slipping to one side, but he seemed unperturbed when we moved it straight again. I realised that his mother had completely disappeared at this point; I suspected she was glad for the break, although the ethos of the clinic is to get the parents involved so they can continue the therapy in their homes.

At 6:00 p.m. I said my goodbyes for the day and walked home. It was the time of the convoy, and all the traffic had been stopped. I cut down a side street, which I hoped went down to the Corniche. It was amazing how walking helped to orientate oneself. This was a part of Luxor that I didn't really know, and walking up one way and back another really helped to get it all into my head. As I had hoped, I came out beside the Nile and had an enjoyable stroll home. It was at this point that I realised I had a scratch on the back of my hand that was bleeding a little. Relieved that my hepatitis and other immunizations were up to date, I reached into my basket for my Milton gel and used copious quantities over the little mark! When I got home, I had a long, long shower. Although the clinic was spotless, sitting on the floor for an hour or so with a dribbling child certainly was the recipe for feeling grubby! I was pleased that I had gone. Although the help I'd given felt minimal, they assured me that they were dependent on their volunteers and that any help was valuable.

The next morning was haircut and colour day! As I had feared, the hairdresser I'd seen the day before greeted me and started the colouring. I was put under the hairdryer for what seemed a lifetime, which worried me intensely—I had never had this experience with a tint before! However, the end result looked promising while my hair was still wet, and he started the cut. This was done almost totally with a razor and scissors that looked like pinking shears! All was going well until he cut himself on the razor! There was much consternation among the girls in the salon until I produced a plaster. I told them I expected a big discount in exchange for this plaster!

There were two Scottish ladies there having henna tattoos done, and there was much hilarity between the two of them.

It was one of the few times I had ever seen anybody else there. There always seemed to be four or five members of staff and no customers! One young man always seemed to be there, but I could never ascertain what he actually did, as he was quite often asleep in a corner!

Finally, I was ready to go. The hairdresser was clearly very proud of his efforts, and everyone agreed it was a very nice colour. The colour *was* fine, despite my original misgivings, and the cut looked promising. But as before, I had the electric shock effect and couldn't wait to get home and get a hairbrush through it!

I went into the kitchen to prepare lunch. The museum kitchen was no longer a source of ready entertainment, as the framework they had been preparing was now covered with a canvas roof and it was no longer possible to see anything. But the canvas did deaden the sound a little and also gave me back the privacy on that balcony; the fact that I could watch them, of course, had meant that they only had to look up to see me, and as I rather enjoyed sitting out there first thing in the morning in my nightie, this particular activity had had to be curtailed!

I ate my lunch and settled down for an afternoon with the computer.

The computer yielded more worrisome news. The tenant of my UK flat had not paid the oil bill, and the oil company was threatening me with legal proceedings! I sent several emails to various people and awaited a response. The agents did not reply at all, and on the second day, I re-sent the original email requesting at least the courtesy of an acknowledgement. My wonderful friend in UK rang the oil company to try to put things off until after Easter, and I waited again to see if the agents would sort this out. Having had my telephone account stopped and my email affected due to a non-payment, I was now facing being blacklisted for credit through no fault of my own. It was maddening!.

The next morning, my haircut did not enhance my mood. It was much worse than I had thought. The fringe and sides were so short that I resembled a coconut, and the colour seemed to have darkened overnight! Ah well, at least it would grow, and I would get used to it.

I spent the morning cleaning, and in the afternoon I set off for my second visit to the clinic. The same little boy was there, and I sat and played with him for a while. Then a new little girl arrived. She was seven, but she looked no more than four. I didn't know how long she had been coming to the clinic, but she was gaining strength and her hands were flattening out beautifully. She had a young mother, who was very involved in her treatment at the clinic and clearly continued the good work at home. Another little boy was also there. He took one look at me and screamed! They told me that he had never seen blond hair before. How I sympathised—I felt exactly like that when I had looked at myself in the mirror that morning! For the latter part of my visit, I was involved in some of the physiotherapy, working the poor little limbs to help strengthen the muscles. The children were uncomplaining and laughed and smiled all the time. It was a very grounding experience.

Good Friday brought an unexpected invitation from my German friend to join her and her son on an outing. We met at about 1:30 p.m. and took a taxi to one of the hotels, where we visited the little zoo. Hundreds of baby bunnies enhanced the Easter feeling and were enchanting to watch. Then we went over the wooden bridge to look at the sleeping crocodile, followed by a donkey ride and feeding the goats. The little boy showed great enthusiasm after the donkey ride to ride the camel, but after they had put the saddle on and he got close, he decided there was no way he was getting on! After much persuasion, I was coerced into taking his place and rode the camel round its enclosure!

The afternoon was incredibly hot—certainly over one hundred degrees—so we retreated to the hotel where we ate ice cream and had cold drinks. We made a quick visit to the playground and then took a brisk walk to the pier to catch the courtesy boat back to Luxor. It took about ten minutes, and my friend's little boy was allowed to sit at the wheel and take charge of the boat—a great achievement at two and a half! The finale to the afternoon was tea at McDonalds, and then we went our separate ways.

Easter Sunday was less eventful. I woke up with a splitting headache, so I took pills and had a shower and a light breakfast. I wanted to go to the post box but didn't feel I could face the heat and the long walk until the headache lifted. I sat quietly for a couple of hours; then, feeling better, I set out for the post box. There was no post for me, but I felt that the walk was good for me, and I decided on lunch out as an Easter Sunday treat.

I had noticed a new café almost directly opposite the flat, right on the Nile, so I tried it. It was excellent. Right at the water's edge, I watched the small fish in the Nile whilst having a cold drink and then ordered a toasted sandwich. The café was beautifully shaded, and they had fans that sprayed water and kept everything nice and cool. My eldest daughter rang whilst I was there, and we chatted all the way through my lunch, making it feel as though she had been having lunch with me!

I had spoken to my younger daughter via the computer just before the Easter holiday, so it was lovely to have touched base with them both and spoken to all the grandchildren. It didn't seem like Easter, my usual timetable being several services to sing at church, too much chocolate, and lots of hot cross buns! The Coptic Christians celebrated Easter, but there was no evidence of it in the shops or in the town. Certainly there were no chocolate eggs, which was probably a good thing! I did miss the hot cross buns; this was probably the first Easter that I hadn't eaten any. Doubtless there would still be some in the supermarket when I got back to the UK, as they seemed to be available through most of the year these days.

I was wondering what Monday would bring, as it was a Muslim holiday celebrating spring. This year it coincided with the Christian Easter, but this was not always the case. Evidently, everybody celebrated spring by going out and picnicking. I was told by friends that every available piece of green was covered with people and that there was inevitably a boating accident when too many people crammed onto boats to get across to the various islands on the Nile! My friends had advised to stay in, but I thought I might pop down to the local hotel and spend the morning round the swimming pool, maybe with lunch there. I would decide in the morning.

In the meantime, I was preoccupied with a house pet I seemed to have acquired: Larry the Lizard! Having been initially reassured that he wasn't the scorpion that one of my guests had thought him to be, I was now finding his presence a bit too much of a good thing. He lived primarily behind the big unit in the sitting room, but as it was getting warmer, he was getting quite lively and rushed around the top of the walls and over the ceilings at an alarming rate. It always made me jump, and I would really prefer he lived outside, but it seemed we were destined to share our living space!

When I checked my email before retiring, I found that the Electricity Board was threatening to cut off my supply because the tenant had not paid the electricity bill. I was horrified! I would have to take all this up through official channels when I returned. This was the third outstanding bill that had caused me problems. I sent a suitable missive to the agents and went to bed.

In the middle of Easter Sunday night, my bad headache turned into a full-blown migraine; it was the only really severe one that I had experienced since being here, which required an injection. Strange that it should have struck when my primary stress levels were concerned with my return to the UK. Having taken pills all through the day, I bit the bullet and gave myself an Imigran injection. I spent a restless night, but the pain eased. By morning, it was just a background headache and a very sore neck, but I felt decidedly fragile.

The morning was not quite so hot, and there was a breeze. I looked out towards the Nile at about 7:00 a.m. and saw lots of Egyptian families already walking along the Corniche and claiming their various pitches. I decided I would go down to the hotel as planned, as it was only a few minutes walk and I could relax in the shade round the pool.

I left home at about 10:00 a.m. and saw with interest all the Egyptian families camped out under every tree along the Corniche. The grass didn't seem to be an issue; it was the shade that was important, and some families were sitting on the pavement under the trees. I arrived at the hotel and found myself a sunbed in the shade. I was glad I had got there so early, as in another hour, the whole place was packed. It had never occurred to me that the hotels would open their doors to everyone on this holiday Monday. Egyptian families made up 90 percent of the crowd, and the pool was full of noisy nine-to-fourteen-year old Egyptian boys. There wasn't a free sunbed anywhere. It was lovely to see them enjoying themselves so much, but it was loud; after my migraine the previous night, loud was not really what I needed!

I decided to investigate the massage opportunities. Whilst I had been at the clinic the previous week, the doctor had told me that he was involved in the massage facilities at various hotels, and this was one of them. A young Muslim girl was behind the desk, and she said she would be happy to do a massage for me now. It was £9 for a half body massage for half an hour. I explained that I had had a very bad headache, and she nodded knowingly. Her massage was just right. Exceedingly gentle and soothing, she massaged my back, shoulders, neck, and head, then turned me over and did the rest of my head and my face. This should definitely be on prescription for migraine sufferers—it was wonderful!

Feeling as if I were walking about six inches above the ground, I found a table at the poolside restaurant for lunch. The waiter came over and leaned towards me

"It is a Christian holiday—Easter!" he told me conspiratorially.

I ordered a calamari sandwich with fries, then indulged in strawberry ice cream. As everything was so full and busy, I then returned home, walking past all the Egyptian families having their picnics. I had a little siesta, then showered and washed my hair. I felt like a new woman! Now if I could just stay in this mode, I could address my various UK problems tomorrow!

After a few days and a series of increasingly strong emails, most of the issues concerning the outstanding tenant's bills in the UK were resolved. The check-out schedule was sent to me, and I was told that as soon as I agreed to this and they could return the tenant's deposit, they would also return my emergency float money which they had been holding. This I did not understand. Why couldn't they release that to me now? The tenancy was finished, the responsibility was again mine, and they had no bills to pay out of my float money. I felt I was being held by ransom over the deposit money. I read the schedule, and there were a couple of things I was anxious about, so I emailed and asked for clarification. As it was a Friday, I was again playing the waiting game before I expected a reply.

I walked down the road to get a topup phone card for my mobile. It is common in Luxor for the locals to throw buckets of water over the pavements outside their shops to keep the dust down. Today, the roads were wet. I was strolling along, enjoying the sunshine, minding my own business, when I passed a large metal gate. As I walked past it, I got drenched! Someone had thrown a bucket of water from the other side! I was so shocked that I shouted, and cries of apology came from the other side of the gate. It was a hot day, and once I got over the shock, I found it quite funny. I was only wet from the waist down, and it would dry in a matter of minutes. I just hoped he had been throwing clean water!

During my next week at the clinic, I met still more new patients, including a gorgeous four-year-old boy with a winning smile and a little chuckle. His mother was young and talked to him all the time, to which he responded well. He did well when strapped into the chair to keep him in a standing position, but when we took him out of it, I realised that he was completely floppy with no control of his spine and little of his neck and head. I also helped with vibration therapy to a little girl's upper limbs to stimulate the muscles, and then with some physiotherapy exercises for an adult woman. On Thursday afternoon, the same little boy was there who had been upset by my blond hair. It had the same effect this time. He took one look at me, and his little face crumpled! I was getting to know the women who regularly worked there, and it was nice to build up a relationship with them, even though so few of them spoke English. We managed to communicate very well, and it was a real pleasure to see them each week.

Another week brought another plumbing problem! The kitchen cold tap was hardly working, and in my endeavour to mend the faulty flush button on the toilet, I broke it completely! The plumber came at 8:00 p.m. He was a different man who spoke a little English and was extremely helpful. He took the cistern apart and showed me that the plastic plunger that worked the button had cracked into two pieces and would need to be replaced. Before he went out to buy the part, he fixed the kitchen tap, and as we passed the other toilet, I heard that it was constantly filling up, so he sorted that out, too. He went off to buy the part, but when he came back, I learned that he'd had to buy a complete set. No matter, he said, next time something went wrong, I would have all the parts! He soon had it fixed, and I paid him a total of £7. I was delighted.

My delight, needless to say, was short-lived, as during the course of the evening I realised that the button was still not working properly. The next morning, I rang the plumber again and arranged a return visit. I didn't think I would ever get used to this multi-visit necessity to get things right, but it didn't worry me as much as it had at the beginning. After all, they always came back in good humour and eventually got it all sorted satisfactorily.

I felt the need for a little retail therapy. There were one or two things I'd had my eye on, but I'd been very self-disciplined about them. On this particular afternoon, my will-power collapsed! I started next door at the museum shop just to look, but I saw a photograph album that matched one I already had. Now this was not impulsive, I told myself, I actually needed this! I asked the price, and it was excessive, so I said so and explained that I lived here, so I knew what the price should be.

"Where do you live?"

"Next door."

"Are you married?"

"Yes."

"To an Egyptian?"

"Yes."

"What is his name?"

Oh no! It was one thing to stray from the truth for the sake of ease, but too many questions became very complicated. I named my "husband" Mohammed, as it would cover at least 75 percent of the male population, and I wouldn't forget it if asked another time! The man was delighted and said that I must have tea with him. Oh, must I, really? Of course, I did, but after tea, he showed me four bracelets, asking me to choose one as a gift. Oh dear, this meant that I had to buy the photograph album and up until then, I could have changed my mind! I chose a bracelet and thanked him, then started back up on the cost of the album. He told me that since I was local, whatever I suggested he would accept. I suggested half of what he'd asked originally; to my amazement, he accepted it!

But it didn't prove to be such a bargain after all. When I took it back home, I realised it was smaller than the other one and would not hold the photographs I needed it to. However, for the price I had paid, I really didn't mind. I would find another way to use it.

I went on to another shop to buy some mugs that I liked. While I was there, it seemed sensible to buy the photograph album that really *did* match the original! I also picked up a lovely letter opener and a greeting card. Excellent. We laughed at the fact that I was such a regular customer, and he threw in the card for free! Why stop there? I would only be here for another three weeks, after all! A crystal palm tree that I had been resisting for days was the next purchase, and with very little effort, I managed to get 15 percent off the price. Then I spotted a little glass Aladdin's lamp. Well, I couldn't leave that behind, as I had recently decided to start a collection of these lamps! Finally, I bought some more plates to match those I was collecting, a new kitchen knife to replace the one whose handle had fallen off, and—oh my goodness—wasn't that a cutlery set that matched exactly the set I had bought over from Sainsburys?

At that point, my conscience kicked in, and I returned home. I was thrilled with all my purchases. The cutlery set wasn't an exact match, but it was so close that no one would notice. The only problem was that when I washed it all to put away, I found that a third of them had loose handles already! The Aladdin's lamp fitted in perfectly with the other two and reminded me of my father, who had also collected them. The new mugs were great, and the additional plates completed the set. What an excellent afternoon!

Midway through April, I realised that the police were now in their white summer uniforms and that the leaves were returning to the trees opposite. It wouldn't be very much longer before a portion of the Nile was obscured again.

My confidence in the plumber turned out to be ill-founded. He returned good naturedly the day after his initial visit, promptly at 7:00 p.m. as arranged. He solved the problem of the constantly running water, but he could not understand my refusal to accept the broken flush button.

"It is not bad," he told me with a smile on his face.

"It is not good, either," was my reply.

He spent considerable time with it and then called me back.

"Try," he instructed me.

I did. There was no change. "We can change the whole mechanism," he told me. This seemed a good idea, so off he went to buy silicone to complete the job. He was gone about half an hour and then spent an hour and a half putting it all together. There were bits all over the bathroom and the little inner hallway. Eventually, he called me back to show me that the new part did not fit my cistern, and he would have to put the old one back. Half an hour later, he asked for a knife, then matches, and finally, sellotape! After three hours, he called me back into the bathroom. He had achieved absolutely nothing! The flush button still did not work, although he told me again that it was "not bad." It was now 10:20 p.m., and I decided that enough was enough. I thanked him, and he made a token gesture at clearing up and then left, telling me confidently that if I had any other problems, I could just call him! I thought, probably not!

I made a quick phone call to a friend to ask if he could find me an alternative plumber in the morning, and then I turned to the considerable mess. The small rug in the hallway was filthy. I had lost track of the number of times plumbing problems had resulted in this poor little rug getting covered in bits of plastic and plumbing materials and soaked. It was a warm night, so working in just a T-shirt, I got cracking. There was debris all over the place, and all the sanitary ware was filthy. Worst of all was the cistern, which was covered in silicone with dirt sticking to it. I couldn't get it off with ordinary cleaner. What could I use? I didn't have any Metholated Spirit, which would have dissolved it in seconds. Then I remembered my nail varnish remover. This might just do it. I tried. It was a lengthy job, needing considerable elbow grease, but I got the worst of it off.

I went to bed feeling tired and disgruntled, hoping that the new day would bring a resolution to the plumbing problem.

I awoke in the morning and decided on a swim. I passed a couple of very pleasant hours and returned home. On my way up the stairs, the little lady who seemed to work for my neighbour two floors down accosted me. She called to her employer, who rushed out.

"Ah, water, water," she said.

My heart sank.

"Come." She beckoned me in. I followed her through her flat to a balcony, and we went outside. She pointed to water on the ground, then pointed up to the pipe coming from my flat, indicating pouring water. I couldn't see any. She spoke practically no English at all, and her Arabic was getting excited. In desperation, I rang an Egyptian friend who did a translation for me. I found out that this lady had a plumber there at the moment, that he was good, and that he would look at my plumbing problems for me. Wonderful!

I was then asked to take a seat and plied with lemonade and biscuits. "With my own hand," she told me, indicating the biscuits.

I dutifully said how good they were, at which point she disappeared into the kitchen, returning with a plate and tin foil. She put together a small parcel of about fifteen biscuits for me! At this point, the plumber came in and we went upstairs to my flat. He saw the problems and said he could fix them. He also showed me the cracked pipe outside, which he could also fix. He needed parts and would return in an hour.

Sure enough, he returned in exactly one hour. He restored the cloakroom toilet in no time, but the bathroom needed more parts, which he would bring tomorrow, when he would also fix the pipe outside. He would come back tomorrow at 2:00 p.m. Oh, I did hope so!

The following day dawned, and I did various chores round the flat. At about 11:30 a.m., I had a shower and washed my hair. Fortunately, I was dressed when I heard the doorbell, but my hair was wet and I had just put mousse in it. I went to the door, and there was the plumber. This was an Egyptian first—two hours early! He came in, indicated the bathroom, and regaled me with a torrent of information in Arabic, finishing with, "friend, phone." He pointed at me.

I rang my friend again, and the translation process began. The plumber had fixed the problem with the pipe outside, but the toilet needed a new part that would cost 5LE, and his fee for sorting out all the problems would be 80LE. If I was happy with this, he would go and get the part and come back and fix it. At 50p for the part and £8 for his fee, I was very happy; so off he went, returning soon afterwards. My hair had dried and was crisp with mousse, and I just had time to resurrect it by the time the plumber returned. He fixed the problem in no time, then called me in to flush the toilet. It was perfect. He was thrilled, as was I. I was instructed to try it again, and his obvious pleasure in my relief was delightful.

There was further excitement that day. I was in the kitchen when I heard an almighty thud that seemed to shake the very core of the building. Heavens! What on earth had happened now? I rushed into the living room and out onto the balcony, as I could hear great commotion outside. A man was up one of the trees opposite, chainsaw in hand, and most of the branches were on the ground. The main branch had just been felled, and that's what had caused the vibration. I noticed that there were parked cars still all around, and I wondered how close some of these branches had come to them! I wasn't too upset about the tree; the main electricity cable was caught up in its branches, so getting rid of it was probably a good idea.

I was not pleased, however, when an hour later I looked out and found the other tree had also gone. Apart from the fact that these beautiful flowering trees were no longer there, the newly open vista offered me no privacy. I could now see straight into the flats across the road—and they into mine. Granted, I now had an unbroken view of the Nile, but I had also lost my shade. The thermometer had gone off the gauge! I had no fear of heights, but sitting at the edge of the balcony with all that space was disconcerting. I supposed I would get used to it. On the upside, the inside of the flat was now considerably lighter and brighter.

It seemed there was never a dull moment, and I wondered what the next source of excitement would be. I didn't have to wait long to find out.

I had been querying my return air ticket since Christmas. I had been told that the Egyptian government ruling was that one could not fly out on a charter ticket if one had been in Egypt for longer than three months. I raised the problem with the travel agent in the UK. He checked and said I would be fine. I was still fearful nonetheless. I had been given the number for the Cosmos office in Luxor, and decided I would check my ticket. The woman in the office confirmed my worst fears: not only did she have no record of my ticket, but I would not be able to fly out on a charter!

A series of phone calls to the travel agent followed. I explained that the error was not mine, and that somebody—I didn't really mind who, but not me!—was going to have to stand the cost of a scheduled flight ticket. The next phone call informed me that all the seats were booked on the date I needed to travel, but that I could go out the following week. This was not good news, as I had to work that day. I said that I would accept it, provided that either the travel agent or Cosmos paid me for my loss of earnings, but I really did not want to lose the work; I would be letting people down, and I did not want a reputation for unreliability. But by the end of the day, I received the phone call I had hoped for. Cosmos had refunded the agent, who had managed to book me a scheduled flight on the day I'd originally intended to travel. The only downside was that I had to fly to Cairo first and transfer to the London flight, which would then take me to Heathrow instead of Gatwick. Never mind, I would cope. I made a quick phone call to my daughter, and we arranged for her husband to collect me from Heathrow and take me straight to their home that Monday evening.

What a day! I felt exhausted, but at least things had been resolved.

The time was passing so quickly. Less than two weeks were left. I felt like something was screaming inside: *don't make me go back, please don't make me go back!* The pull of friends and family was great, and I was looking forward to seeing everyone, but it was going to be so hard to leave friends behind in Luxor. I was really excited about seeing my elder daughter and my youngest granddaughter immediately on my return, then seeing my younger daughter and her little family a month later when they returned from Australia. I had missed my friends and the girlie chats, and it would be lovely to catch up with everyone, but there was still the pull of Egypt. I felt I had just scratched the surface, and just as I was beginning to feel really settled, it was time to leave.

I was starting to do a round of goodbyes and had lunch with my Australian friend. She took me to a restaurant in an old house in Luxor. It was a treasure chest of old furniture and furnishings, with individual rooms for private dining, a big, covered terrace upstairs, and a small courtyard garden. We had a leisurely, delightful lunch in these wonderful surroundings.

We parted company at the restaurant, and I started my walk home via the bookshop. It was a stiflingly hot afternoon, and I picked my way down the dusty street, negotiating my way round some innovative driving! As I approached the main square behind the temple, a taxi pulled up in front of me, making it impossible for me to walk past. I looked up and found it to be the driver I used, with an English couple I knew as passengers! They had arrived the day before, and I was thrilled to see them. I stopped for a quick chat before we went our separate ways.

I bought myself a new book and continued home, stopping for a cold drink at the café opposite the flat. The waiter was pleased to see me again, but in his enthusiasm, he dropped my drink, which dripped relentlessly into my lap! He was mortified, but it would dry in no time in the heat. After my drink, I wandered past the shops tailored toward cruise ship passengers. Amongst them was a leather shop, and I stopped to enquire about some sandals. My current leather flip-flops were about to break, and I wanted to replace them. The price started at £22, which was laughable, and with very little effort I bought them for £8. My pleasure was short-lived: I put them on to wander round the flat, and wearing them was agony! This was not a bargain; this was a huge mistake!

Larry the Lizard was still very much in evidence, scurrying around the edge of the ceilings. We had a wonderful moment when I went to open the curtains and found him on the window on the other side. It seemed to happen in slow motion. We looked at each other, his little eyes quite clearly looking straight into mine. Then as I exclaimed out loud, it was as though he had, too! We both jumped, and he flew off, disappearing behind the furniture. He appeared an hour or so later in the top corner of the room, where one of his little legs got caught in a cobweb. He shook his foot; I could almost hear him saying, "Yuck, what is this?"

He scurried away, then shook his foot again; it was clearly an unpleasant experience for him! I was getting used to him being there, and he was definitely less worrying now that I had given him a name!

With a little over a week left, I was awaiting the arrival of some urgent papers from the UK that were being sent by DHL. I was tracking their progress on the Internet. They left England on Monday and were supposed to be with me on Wednesday. However, I saw no progress online on Tuesday. I emailed customer services inquiring about my post. Then I went to the post box on Wednesday, only to find everything closed up because it was a national holiday. On Thursday morning, I received an email from customer services, telling me about the national holiday and that my post would arrive on Saturday. However, they could not deliver to a post box address, only to my home. This worried me. Nobody could ever find my flat; the street did not have a name, which was why I had set up the box number in the first place. I rang the number I'd been given in the Cairo DHL office and spoke to a lovely lady who took all the details and assured me that the courier would ring me if he could not find me. I emailed customer service with the same information just to make sure, suggesting that they might like to make a small refund under the circumstances. This post had cost a staggering £65 and was supposed to reach me in three days. And now, I was less than confident that I was actually going to receive it. I supposed if worse came to worst, I could always meet the courier outside the museum!

I felt stir crazy. It had taken most of the day to sort out the package situation, and I felt the need to go out. I popped out at the end of the afternoon for a few odds and ends, but lacked enthusiasm to do anything else. I had intended to walk up to the clinic to say goodbye and drop off a big bag of sweets that I had bought for them all, but motivation escaped me, and I decided to put it off until next week. I had many things to do and people to say goodbye to in my remaining ten days, and the sadness of all these impending goodbyes was undoubtedly the cause of my lethargy.

May

Only a few precious days left, and so much to do.

There seemed to be an endless round of goodbyes. I hadn't realised just how many people I had got to know during my seven months in Luxor. I was also beginning to panic about how I was going to get everything into one suitcase when it had taken three to get everything here! Of course, I was leaving many things behind. My computer printer had taken up a lot of space, and that was staying; but I found myself wondering why I had packed so many pairs of shoes!

In the midst of everything, I discovered that the money I was transferring to Egypt had not gone; after countless phone calls, I was told that if I could find a bank that dealt with the Royal Bank of Scotland, then the money could be transferred in two days. I was particularly anxious that it come through before my return, as the last time I had transferred money it had got "lost in transit" and taken weeks to sort out. It was therefore important that I was still here when it was supposed to arrive so I could check that it really was here. I decided that HSBC would be a good starting point. It was a newly opened bank in Luxor, and of course also in England.

I arrived promptly at the bank at 9:00 a.m., only to find that they didn't open until 9:30 a.m. I went next door to the hotel and sat in the cool for half an hour. At 9:30 a.m., I went back, and the man behind the glass indicated that they weren't open yet. I looked for shade; it was scorching even at this time in the morning. The only shade available was by the police point, so I went to stand there. Immediately one of the policemen started chatting, and it at least passed the time. After five minutes, I returned to the door of the bank; they still weren't open. I looked at my watch; they really should have been opened. I ambled down to sit on a little wall, and two minutes later the door opened and the doorman came looking for me.

Inside was cool and calm. I was introduced to someone who would look after me. I explained my problem, and he said they did deal with the Royal Bank of Scotland: in fact, they used to be part of it. Excellent. This man had lived and worked in Kensington High Street and Brighton, and his English was excellent. Similarly, his knowledge of the English system was helpful. In no time at all, my account was opened, and sure enough, two days later my funds had been transferred.

It seemed silly to keep my other Egyptian bank account open when I was no longer going to use it. The next day I went in to close the account.

"Why do you want to do that?" I was asked.

"Because I don't use it."

"Oh."

It took only a few moments, and I left with an English fifty-pound note in my hand—the entire contents of that account. I was pleased with my decision. They were very nice in that bank, but they spoke very little English, and whilst one lady recognised me, she did not know my name. My new "account manager" on the other hand, had my mobile number registered in his phone, addressed me by my first name, and spoke excellent English—and there didn't seem to be any problem in moving funds from one account to another. This surely had to be the way forward.

I walked up to the clinic on Tuesday afternoon to say goodbye. I hadn't been in to help for a week as there had been so much to do, so I took the large bag of sweets and set off. It was still excessively hot at 4:30 p.m., but I walked slowly and took water with me. I arrived and cursed my lack of thought. It was May Day, a bank holiday, and the clinic was closed! I turned and walked back, stopping to buy a packet of biscuits on the way. The man asked me if I had a cold because I had a red nose! Obviously my nose was reflecting the intense heat! I got home after being out for only half an hour. I felt exhausted and had a splitting headache. I let myself cool down gently before turning on the air-conditioning and made sure I drank plenty of water. The temperature must have been about 104, and half an hour walking in that temperature, even in the shade, was heavy going.

I resolved the next day to get a taxi up to the clinic, arranging for it to wait for me and take me on into town. This time we left at 5:30 p.m. The girls at the clinic were delighted to see me.

"Where have you been?"

I explained that I had been busy, and that I was returning to England on Monday, but that I would see them the next time I was back. It was an emotional goodbye: hugs and kisses all round and lots of photos. The girls all wanted to see themselves in the photo, and there was much laughter. I hadn't realised how much I would miss them.

The taxi drove me into town, and I said goodbye to the driver, too. I went quickly to the baker to get a few rolls to last me until I left. He was pleased to see me.

"Welcome back."

And when I left, he called "Goodbye, habibi!"

Heavens, I was even sad to say goodbye to the baker! Next I went to see my Australian friend in her shop. We had a long chat, and I bought a couple things from her. I had got to know the people in the local shops very well, and I stopped by to have a cup of tea and say goodbye there.

A lot of the stress I'd experienced recently was because I'd made the decision to sell my UK flat and buy something smaller. This would enable me to come to Egypt more often and be more of a "hands on" granny with my family when I was in the UK. I had been accepted on to the bank of the hospital where I had worked before for many years, so I had work to come back to; but without the commitment of a full-time job, I would have the flexibility I now required. Having put the flat on the market, I had an offer on it within eight days! On top of that, they were anxious to complete the sale in two-to-three months! I accepted the offer, aware that it could still all fall through, and even more aware that I must find another home.

I trawled the Internet and sent emails to agents, setting up places to view immediately when I returned. It was exciting, but scary, too. There would be so very much to do as soon as I got back. The start of another whole new chapter of my life was about to begin.

I had another day of emotional farewells when I met my German friend and her little boy for lunch. I invited them back to the flat, and we bought cold drinks and ice creams on the way. As we were leaving the restaurant, my usual taxi driver was driving along, and he stopped to talk to us. We hopped in the taxi, and he drove us back to the flat. My friend and I chatted for a couple of hours, and then it was time for her to go. I felt the tears pricking. She had been so kind and helpful, and it was hard to say goodbye, despite the fact that I knew I would be back in the autumn. I was hoping the sale of my big flat in the UK and impending purchase of something smaller would enable me to make other long visits to Egypt in the years ahead, but so much was still uncertain.

Earlier in the day I had started laying out some things for packing. It became apparent quite quickly that I was not going to get this all into one case. I rang Egyptair to see if I could pre-book and pay for excess baggage, but was told it must be done at check-in. I asked if it would be a problem to have two cases. Whilst I was told that it would be alright, I was not convinced and started to worry about how I was going to get these two cases back to England at the same time. A travel agent in England had told me that if the plane was full, one of the cases would be put on a different flight and I would have to collect it the next day. This called for some strategic packing, just in case.

I had two days in Egypt left. I gave myself a "chill out" day and tried to relax. I started with a swim at the hotel. The water was unusually warm, and it was wonderful. I followed it with a massage. The masseuse who had been so relaxing and gentle when I went the first time with a headache had turned into a warrior! It was agony! I tried to convince myself that this was doing me good, but I couldn't say it was relaxing! I changed and went to have lunch by the pool. I found a nice table in the shade, and the service was quick. Next I went in for a hair-do. The hairdresser was, yet again, one I had never seen before, but he turned out to be the best of the bunch! Finally, I had a manicure and a pedicure, and I emerged, totally pampered. I went home for a shower and change of clothes and then went out to dinner with a friend. It was a lovely day in preparation for the mayhem of the following one, when I must pack and close everything up, ready to leave at 7:00 a.m. on Monday morning.

I went to have a shower. The weather was constantly hot now, usually forty degrees and sometimes higher. As a result, it was very difficult to have a cool shower. The water pipes went up the outside of the building, and when the weather was very hot, the water heated in the pipes before it reached the taps. Even running the water for five minutes didn't always do the trick. It had caught me out many times, and it made rinsing contact lenses a nightmare. So, having a hotter shower than I would have chosen, I got ready for my last evening of relaxation before my journey back to the UK.

It was a lovely evening, punctuated with one last water event! As I was walking down the street with my friend, a young girl threw some water out. I wasn't looking her way, so I had no idea what she was throwing until the water hit me at shoulder level, catching my face, hair, and everything from the waist up on my right side! I was soaked! Memories of my previous soaking came to mind—I obviously attracted water throwers like a magnet!

Next day, I went to the post office for a last-minute check of the post box, on to the bank, then home. I then faced the daunting task of packing and cleaning. I defrosted the fridge, which only took about twenty minutes in the heat, did my last load of washing, and generally cleared up.

It was a sad time. Tears were near the surface continually, and every now and then I had a little weep. Text messages from my daughter and friends compounded the fragility of my emotions. I was so looking forward to seeing my friends and family in England, but leaving all this behind was heart rending. I had suspected it would be hard, but it was worse than I had anticipated. I felt sick with the thought of leaving, even though I knew I would be back. It was hard to be positive. I knew I had an exciting, albeit stressful, time ahead with the impending move, and I kept reminding myself that this was the way forward to spending other years like this one, with the winter in Egypt and the summer in England. So taking myself firmly in hand, I progressed with the task of packing up, ready for my early morning start to the airport the next day.

The Return

I awoke without difficulty the next morning and made my final round of closing everything down. The car arrived early to collect me, and I closed and locked the front door for the final time. Upon arrival at check-in, the man behind the desk told me he would not charge me excess baggage on this part of the flight, as he was quite sure they would charge me at Cairo. I was delighted. I bought myself breakfast, staggered by the cost of a coffee and a stale roll. Soon I was on the plane to Cairo; as it took off, I felt the tears rolling down my cheeks. Oh, this was much, much harder than I had anticipated.

At Cairo, I bumped into someone I knew from Luxor. It was good to see her, and we chatted whilst awaiting our luggage at the carousel. Having retrieved my two cases and said goodbye, I found a porter who helped me to the international terminal, where I had to check in again for London. Heart in mouth, I waited to see how much excess baggage I would be charged; to my amazement, my two bags were checked straight through with no mention of extra cost!

The rest of my journey passed uneventfully, and at Heathrow, my son-in-law was at the barrier waiting for me. He drove me to their home, where my daughter and granddaughter were waiting at the door. How I had missed them! I spent a few days with them, during which time I retrieved my car from friends and thankfully found I still remembered how to drive!

Then I went back to Sussex. The flat felt strange without all my personal things and with the feeling that someone else had been living there. It made it easy to consider a move, and I wasted no time flat hunting.

It was lovely to meet up with all my friends, and there were many happy times and lovely welcomes. It was the people I had missed, not the place. If I could move my family and all my friends to Luxor with me, I would never come back to the UK! I still had the joy of reunion with my younger daughter and her family to come, as they were due home from their year in Australia in a few weeks.

The high cost of living was as much of a shock as I had anticipated. Coffee and a cake for £3—good heavens, I could have a wonderful dinner out for that in Luxor! A panini and a smoothie at lunch whilst shopping was £6.40—outrageous! A tank of petrol for £37—scandalous! A small punnet of strawberries for £1.99—unbelievable!

I went back to work at the hospital, and I had lots of work booked through the summer, which was a relief. I enjoyed working again and was ready for some mental challenges and companionship.

The sale of the flat was progressing, as was the purchase of the new one. I kept my fingers crossed that it would all go through without too many hitches or too much stress. I had moments of doubt, but I knew in my heart that this was the way forward. This would enable me to divide my life between the family I loved and my working life and friends in England, and my home, life, and friends in Egypt.

Perhaps the best was yet to come. I could feel the sparkle in my soul at the thought of it. The adventure was just beginning. Watch this space!

Post Script

It seemed an important part of the whole experience to consider everything and to remember all the things that annoyed or irritated me, as well as those that gladdened my heart. I therefore started keeping a note of all the things I would miss—and also those that I definitely would NOT.

Things I will Miss
My Egyptian friends
The call to prayer
The children in the school next door when they first arrived and sang, although when they are on holiday, it is even nicer!
The sunshine
Not having to worry about an umbrella or whether to take a coat
The peace of mind and the general feeling of well being
The slow pace of life
Having no demands on my time
The palm trees
The friendliness of people as you walk down the street
The ready availability and cheap prices of the tradesmen
The low cost of living
The fact that everybody genuinely wants to help, even when you don't require it!

Things I will NOT Miss
The shoddy workmanship
The hit-and-miss functioning of everything
THE DUST
The plumbing problems
Taking a taxi to go shopping
Walking up four flights of stairs to get home
Carrying the weekly shop up these four flights of stairs!

Not being able to get things when I need them—just because they are in the shop one week, doesn't mean to say that they will be the next!

Egyptian time-keeping: 9:30 could be 9:15 or 9:45 or any other variation!

The children in the school!

Lightning Source UK Ltd.
Milton Keynes UK
31 October 2009

145686UK00001B/1/P